The Darkest Part of the Night

Zodwa Nyoni

T0026853

methuen | drama

LONDON · NEW YORK · OXFORD · NEW DELHI · SYDNEY

METHUEN DRAMA
Bloomsbury Publishing Plc
50 Bedford Square, London, WC1B 3DP, UK
1385 Broadway, New York, NY 10018, USA
29 Earlsfort Terrace, Dublin 2, Ireland

BLOOMSBURY, METHUEN DRAMA and the Methuen
Drama logo are trademarks of Bloomsbury Publishing Plc

First published in Great Britain 2022

A catalogue record for this book is available from the British Library.

Library of Congress Control Number: 2022941035

ISBN: PB: 978-1-3503-4177-7
ePDF: 978-1-3503-4178-4
eBook: 978-1-3503-4179-1

Series: Modern Plays

Typeset by Mark Heslington Ltd, Scarborough, North Yorkshire

To find out more about our authors and books visit
www.bloomsbury.com and sign up for our newsletters.

Kiln Theatre presents

THE DARKEST PART OF THE NIGHT

By **Zodwa Nyoni**

14 July – 13 August 2022 | Kiln Theatre

CAST
(in alphabetical order)

**Mr Campbell /
Police Officer /
Prison Officer**
James Clyde

Young Shirley
Brianna Douglas

Calvin / Leroy
Andrew French

Anna
Hannah Morrish

Dwight
Lee Phillips

Shirley / Josephine
Nadia Williams

CREATIVE TEAM

Writer
Zodwa Nyoni

Director
Nancy Medina

Designer
Jean Chan

Lighting Designer
Guy Hoare

Sound Designer
Elena Peña

Casting Director
Briony Barnett CDG

Movement Director
Ingrid Mackinnon

**Production
Dramatherapist**
Samantha E Adams

**Voice & Dialect
Coach**
Eleanor Manners

**Costume
Supervisor**
Megan
Keegan-Pilmoor

Wigs Supervisor
Keisha Banya

Fight Director
Kate Waters

Assistant Director
Stephen Bailey

PRODUCTION TEAM

**Production
Manager**
Tom Lee

**Company Stage
Manager**
EJ Saunders

**Deputy Stage
Manager**
Constance Oak

**Assistant
Stage Manager
(Book Cover)**
Aiman Bandali

**Technician /
Lighting Operator**
Eilidh MacKenzie

Wardrobe Manager
Anuccia Botto

**Access All Areas
Creative Support
Workers**
Patricia Hitchcock
Selena Kelly

**Production
Electrician**
Andrew Taylor

**Production
Carpenter**
Tony Forrester

**Lighting
Programmer**
Tamykha Patterson

Set built by
Footprint Scenery
Kiln Theatre
Workshop
The Revolving Stage
Company

SPECIAL THANKS

Access All Areas
David Butler
Calum Walker
Kieran Watson
White Light

CAST

JAMES CLYDE
MR CAMPBELL / POLICE OFFICER / PRISON OFFICER

Theatre credits include: *Tamburlaine, Tartuffe, Timon of Athens, King Lear, Cymbeline, Matilda, Romeo and Juliet, Days of Significance, Comedy of Errors, Twelfth Night* (Royal Shakespeare Company); *Touch* (Soho Theatre); *In the Depths of Dead Love* (Print Room); *Hamlet, Jane Eyre, The Art of Random Whistling* (Young Vic Theatre); *As You Like It, Hedda Gabler, Tobaccoland, The Candidate, Misfits, The Tempest, A Taste of Honey, Macbeth* (Royal Exchange, Manchester); *Twelfth Night, Hang* (National Theatre); *Much Ado About Nothing* (Dubai Opera House); *The Cutting Edge* (Arcola Theatre); *God of Carnage, School for Wives* (Nuffield Theatre); *Dangerous Lady* (Theatre Royal Stratford East); *The Illusion* (Southwark Playhouse); *Single Spies* (Watermill); *Macbeth* (Shakespeare's Globe); *Caucasian Chalk Circle, Jane Eyre, After Mrs Rochester* (Shared Experience / West End); *Absolute Beginners* (Lyric Hammersmith); *I Just Stopped By to See the Man* (Octagon Theatre Bolton); *Ying Tong* (West Yorkshire Playhouse / West End); *The Lucky Ones, The Eleventh Commandment, A Going Concern* (Hampstead Theatre); *A Model Girl* (Greenwich Theatre); *All for Love, A Hard Heart* (Almeida Theatre); *Dreaming* (Queen's Theatre); *Jack's Out* (Bush Theatre); *The Gentleman from Olmedo* (Gate Theatre); *Hated Nightfall, Wounds to The Face* (Royal Court Theatre); *The Castle* (Riverside); *The Ecstatic Bible* (Adelaide Festival); *Scenes from An Execution* (Barbican).

Television credits include: *The Forgiving Earth, Leonardo, Above Suspicion: Deadly Intent, New Tricks, Boudicca, The Bill, London Bridge, Made in Heaven, Maigret, Mr. Thomas, Cluedo, Back Up, In Suspicious Circumstances, Between the Lines.*

Film credits include: *Beauty, Anonymous, The Honeytrap, Cheese, Croupier, Your Night Tonight, Prick Up Your Ears, Glitch, Inheritance.*

Radio credits include: *Ying Tong: A Walk With the Goons, Anthony and Cleopatra: Make Death Love Me.*

Video game credits include: *Battlefield Gothic Armada, Nioh, Codestrike, Witcher 3: Wild Hunt.*

BRIANNA DOUGLAS
YOUNG SHIRLEY

Brianna trained at ALRA North.

Theatre credits include: *Beyond These Walls* (Northern Broadsides / Sheffield Crucible); *A Christmas Carol* [Filmed] (Octagon Theatre Bolton); *Advent Plays* (Oldham Coliseum); *Dead Certain, Unseemly Woman* (Hope Mill Theatre); *Hamlet* (Girl Gang / Hopemill); *Play Box – Brit Bred* [R&D] (Box of Tricks); *Our Loud* [R&D] (Middle Child); *Spank, Mix Tape* [R&D] (Tamasha Theatre); *Pure* [Filmed] (HER Productions).

Television credits include: *Emmerdale, Coronation Street* (ITV).

Brianna will be appearing as Olive Morris in short film *The Ballad of Olive Morris* releasing in mid/late 2022.

ANDREW FRENCH
CALVIN / LEROY

Theatre credits include: *Jitney* (Leeds Playhouse); *Romeo and Juliet* (Regent's Park Open Air Theatre); *The Winter's Tale* (Royal Shakespeare Company); *Two Trains Running* (UK tour); *While We're Here, I Like Mine With A Kiss* (Bush Theatre); *This Flesh Is*

Mine/When Nobody Returns (Border Crossings); *The Iphegenia Quartet* (The Gate); *Bully Boy* (Mercury Theatre Colchester); *Boi Boi is Dead, Refugee Boy* (West Yorkshire Playhouse); *The Initiate/Our Teacher is a Troll* (Roundabout Season, Paines Plough); *Julius Caesar, Romeo and Juliet* (Royal Shakespeare Company); *Measure for Measure* (Almeida Theatre); *Monster* (Royal Exchange Manchester); *As You Like It* (West End); *Reference To Salvador Dali...* (Arcola/Young Vic Theatre); *The Taming of the Shrew, The Tempest* (Nottingham Playhouse Theatre); *The Merchant of Venice, Troilus and Cressida* (National Theatre); *The Merchant of Venice, The Honest Whore* (Shakespeare's Globe Theatre); *Things Fall Apart* (West Yorkshire Playhouse/Royal Court Theatre); *The Tempest* (Shared Experience).

Television credits include: *Temple* (Sky); *A Very English Scandal* (BBC); *Marvin Can't Fail* (Hat Trick); *Capital* (Kudos for BBC 1); *EastEnders, Holby City, Doctors, Causalty* (BBC); *Perfect Parents* (ITV); *Primeval* (Impossible Pictures/ITV); *Soundproof, Blast!* (Films/BBC2); *The Bill* (Thames); *Trust* (Box TV); *In Deep* (Valentine Productions); *A Touch of Frost* (Yorkshire Television); *Family Affairs* (Channel 5); *Burnside* (Thames); *Tough Love* (Granada).

Film credits include: *Artificial Horizon* (Artificial Horizon Limited); *Breaking the Bank* (Black Hangar Studios); *Song for Marion* (WH Films); *Assassination Games* (MPCA Films); *Exorcist: The Beginning* (Morgan Creek); *Exorcist, Dominion* (Morgan Creek USA); *The Merchant of Venice* (BBC Films); *Doctor Sleep* (Kismet Films); *Tailor of Panama* (Columbia Pictures).

Radio credits include: *Doctor Who: Original Sin* (Big Finish Productions); *The Mother Of...* (BBC Radio 4); *The Last Supper* (BBC Radio 3).

HANNAH MORRISH
ANNA

Theatre credits include: *Cancelling Socrates, Hole* (Jermyn Street Theatre); *Renaissance* (Sotto Voce); *All's Well That Ends Well* (Guildford Shakespeare Company & Jermyn Street Theatre); *Antony and Cleopatra* [Ian Charleson Award, Second Prize] (National Theatre); *Coriolanus, Titus Andronicus, Julius Caesar* (RSC); *Arms and the Man* (Watford Palace Theatre); *Flowering Cherry* (Troupe/Finborough Theatre); *A Little Hotel on the Side* (Theatre Royal Bath).

Television credits include: *Father Brown, Call the Midwife.*

Film credits include: *Ceres* (Short), *Nell and Pauline* (Short), *Magpie, No More Kings* (Short), *Arcade* (Short).

LEE PHILLIPS
DWIGHT

Lee is an Associate Artist of Access All Areas. He graduated from Access All Areas' Performance Making Diploma at the Royal Central School of Speech and Drama in 2014.

Theatre credits include: *Fix Us* (INK Festival Soho Theatre, Edinburgh Fringe with BareFace Collective); *unReal City* (Brighton Dome with Access All Areas and Dreamthinkspeak); *The Interrogation* (Access All Areas); *Viva the Live* (ZU-UK); *All Wrapped Up* (Oily Cart UK tour); *The Trial* (Access All Areas and Retz (now Rift) Theatre); *Eye Queue Hear* (Access All Areas UK tour).

Lee is a member of both the BareFace Collective and the collective duo Everyday Daylee. In 2019 Everyday Daylee performed their debut show *#crazyfuturelove* as part of the Occupy Festival at Battersea Arts Centre, and at various festivals and gigs including Bubble Club and the Autism Arts Festival, University of Kent.

Lee also performs with London Bubble, Sardines Dance, Blink Dance Theatre and Entelechy Arts.

NADIA WILLIAMS
SHIRLEY / JOSEPHINE

Theatre credits include:
Anansi's Big Adventure (Bristol Old Vic); *Top Girls, I'm Not Running* (National Theatre); *A Midsummer Night's Dream* (Shakespeare at the Tobacco Factory); *Phaedra's Love* (Bristol Old Vic / Barbican); *After the Accident* (Theatre West); *Trade It?* (Show Of Strength Theatre); *The Curious Incident of the Dog in the Night-Time* (tour – National Theatre).

As Assistant Director: *The Meaning of Zong* (Bristol Old Vic).

Television credits include: *Disclaimer* (Apple TV); *Riches* (Amazon / ITV); *The Crown* (Netflix); *Doctors, Extras, Casualty* (BBC); *Broadchurch* (Kudos).

Film credits include: *Breaking Point* (Sky); *Daylight Rules* (Sky); *Pickney* (Blak Wave); *Carnival* (123 Media).

Radio credits include: *Poetry Please, Positive, Black and White Riot, The Chosen One* (BBC Radio 4).

CREATIVES

ZODWA NYONI
WRITER

Zodwa Nyoni is a Zimbabwean-born writer who has written for theatre, film and television.

The Darkest Part of the Night was a finalist for both the George Devin Award and the Alfred Fagon Award in 2022. Zodwa won the Channel 4 Playwright's Scheme with her play, *Boi Boi is Dead* and was a finalist for the international Susan Smith Blackburn Prize 2014/15.

Plays include: *Nine Lives* (Oran Mór); *Phone Home* (Upstart Theatre, Pathos München & Highway Productions); *Borderline* (Young Vic Theatre); *Ode to Leeds* (Leeds Playhouse); *Duty* (Paines Plough & National Trust); *Beneath the City* (Upstart Theatre); *The Happiness Project* (Pilot Theatre); *The Survivors' Guide To Living* (Young Company: Royal Exchange Manchester).

Zodwa has written two radio plays, *A Khoisan Woman* (Drama on 3) and *Love Again* (BBC Radio 3).

Her first short film *Mahogany* was commissioned by National Trust and 24 Design. This was followed by *Notes On Being A Lady* (Tyneside Cinema / BBC Arts) and *The Ancestors* (BBC Films / BFI Film Hub North).

NANCY MEDINA
DIRECTOR

Nancy Medina is originally from Brooklyn NY, and currently based in Bristol. She is Co-Artistic Director of the Bristol School of Acting in partnership with Tobacco Factory Theatres. She is currently a recipient of the National Theatre's Peter Hall Director's Bursary.

For Kiln: *The Half God of Rainfall* (also Fuel / Birmingham Rep).

Directing credits include: *Moreno* (Theatre503); *Trouble in Mind* (National

Theatre); *Pigeon English* (Tobacco Factory Theatres); *The Laramie Project* (Bristol Old Vic); *Two Trains Running* (Royal & Derngate / English Touring Theatre); *Strange Fruit* (Bush Theatre); *Collective Rage: A Play in 5 Betties* (Royal Welsh College of Music and Drama); *When They Go Low* (NT Connections / Sherman Theatre); *Yellowman* (Young Vic Theatre); *Romeo and Juliet, As You Like it* (GB Theatre); *Curried Goat and Fish Fingers* (Bristol Old Vic); *Dogtag* (Theatre West); *Strawberry & Chocolate, Dutchman* (Tobacco Factory Theatres); *Persistence of Memory* (Rondo Theatre).

JEAN CHAN
DESIGNER

Jean Chan studied at the Royal Welsh College of Music and Drama, graduating in 2008 with a BA (Hons) Degree in Theatre Design. She went on to work as a resident designer, part of the Royal Shakespeare Company's Trainee Design Programme 2008–9. In 2009 she won the Linbury Prize for Stage Design.

For Kiln: *Reasons You Should(n't) Love Me.*

Theatre credits include: *Twelfth Night, A Midsummer Night's Dream* (Shakespeare's Globe); *Open Mic* (ETT / Soho Theatre); *Wild Goose, Plastic* (Theatre Royal Bath); *Much Ado About Nothing* (Shakespeare at the Tobacco Factory); *This Girl Laughs, This Girl Cries, This Girl Does Nothing* (Stellar Quines, Scottish tour); *The Hired Man* (Queen's Theatre, Hornchurch); *Dick Whittington, Jack and the Beanstalk* (Lyric Hammersmith); *Plastic* (Ustinov, Bath Theatre Royal); *Working, The Hairy Ape, The Irish Giant, The Seagull* (Southwark Playhouse); *Ticking* (Trafalgar Studios); *The Witches, James and the Giant Peach, The BFG* (Dundee Rep); *Jumpy, Hedda Gabler* (The Royal Lyceum, Edinburgh); *The Season Ticket* (Pilot Theatre and Northern Stage); *Cyrano de Bergerac* (Royal & Derngate and Northern Stage); *Mother Courage, Bordergames, Tonypandemonium* (National Theatre Wales).

Opera credits include: *La Calisto* (Longborough Opera Festival).

Costume designs include: *Legally Blonde* (Regent's Park Open Air Theatre); *Knights' Tale* (Toho Theatre, Japan); *The Grinning Man* (Trafalgar Studios and Bristol Old Vic); *Aladdin* (Lyric Hammersmith); *Lionboy* (Complicité).

GUY HOARE
LIGHTING DESIGNER

For Kiln: *Wife, Reasons You Should(n't) Love Me, The Wife of Willesden.*

Theatre credits include: *Sea Wall / A Life* (Broadway); *Julie, The Deep Blue Sea, Here We Go, Strange Interlude* (National Theatre); *Jesus Hopped the A Train, Wings, A Doll's House, World Factory, Far Away* (Young Vic Theatre); *One For Sorrow, NSFW, In Basildon* (Royal Court Theatre); *Roots, Serenading Louie, Be Near Me* (Donmar Warehouse); *Little Revolution, A Delicate Balance, Waste* (Almeida Theatre); *Clarence Darrow* (The Old Vic); *The Father, Othello* (West End); *Peter Pan* (National Theatre of Scotland); *Sleeping Beauty* (Citizens Theatre); *Cock* (Chichester Festival Theatre); *Macbeth, As You Like It* (West Yorkshire Playhouse); *West Side Story, Grease* (Curve); *Assassins* (Crucible, Sheffield), *A Christmas Carol* (Birmingham Repertory Theatre); *Kes* (Liverpool Playhouse); *Going Dark* (Sound & Fury).

Designs for dance include: Arthur Pita's *The Metamorphosis* (Royal Opera House / Joyce Theatre, New York | Southbank Award for Dance) and Mark Bruce's *Dracula* (Wilton's Music Hall | Southbank Award for Dance), and various pieces worldwide for – amongst others – Rafael Bonachela, Christopher Bruce, Dan Daw, Shobana Jeyasingh, Akram Khan and Alexander Whitley. He also designed *Mischief* and *The Global Playground* for Theatre Rites and several cross-artform works for Gandini Juggling.

Opera credits include: *The Firework-Maker's Daughter* (Royal Opera House); *Jakob Lenz* (ENO); *American Lulu* (Bregenz Festival); *King Priam, Paul Bunyan* (English Touring Opera | Olivier Award for Outstanding Achievement in Opera).

ELENA PEÑA
SOUND DESIGNER

For Kiln: *Reasons You Should(n't) Love Me, Snowflake, The Kilburn Passion, Arabian Nights.*

Theatre credits include: *Two Palestinians Go Dogging, Maryland, seven methods of killing kylie jenner, Living Newspaper* (Royal Court Theatre); *The Chairs, Mass Observation* (Almeida Theatre); *Trouble in Mind* (National Theatre); *Open Mic* (ETT & Soho Theatre); *Antigone, Women of Troy* (LAMDA); *Nora: A Doll's House, Rockets & Blue Lights, Brainstorm* (National Theatre); *Macbeth, Mountains* (Royal Exchange, Manchester); *Autoreverse, Boat* (BAC); *Everything* (Company Three); *Misty* (West End), *Going Through, Hir, Islands* (Bush Theatre); *The Memory of Water* (Nottingham Playhouse); *The Remains of the Day* (Out of Joint / Royal & Derngate, Northampton); *Thick as Thieves* (Clean Break); *The Wizard of Oz* (Pitlochry Festival); *All of Me* (China Plate); *Double Vision* (Wales Millennium Centre); *The Caretaker* (Bristol Old Vic); *The Lounge* (Soho / Summer Hall, Edinburgh); *How I Hacked My Way Into Space* (Unlimited / UK tour); *Years of Sunlight* (Theatre503); *The Bear / The Proposal, Flashes* (Young Vic Theatre); *Sleepless* (Analogue / Staatstheater Mainz, Germany); *The Christians* (Traverse); *I Call My Brothers, The Iphigenia Quartet, Unbroken* (Gate Theatre); *Thebes Land, Ant Street, Brimstone and Treacle, Knives In Hens* (Arcola Theatre); *You Have Been Upgraded* (Unlimited / Science Museum); *Seochon Odyssey* (HiSeoul Festival, Korea).

Dance credits include: *Patrias, Quimeras* (Sadler's Wells / Paco Peña Flamenco Company).

Television / online credits include: *Have Your Circumstances Changed?, Brainstorm, The Astro Science Challenge.*

Radio credits include: *Rockets and Blue Lights, The Meet Cute, Twelve Years, Duchamp's Urinal.*

Installation credits include: *Have Your Circumstances Changed?, Yes These Eyes are the Windows* (ArtAngel).

Awards include: Offie On Comm Award for Best Audio Production (*Rockets and Blue Lights*).

Elena is an Associate Artist for Inspector Sands.

BRIONY BARNETT CDG
CASTING DIRECTOR

For Kiln / Tricycle: *NW Trilogy, When the Crows Visit, White Teeth, Half God of Rainfall* (also Birmingham Rep); *Handbagged* (also West End); *The Invisible Hand, Ben Hur, A Wolf in Snakeskin Shoes, The House that Will Not Stand, The Colby Sisters, One Monkey Don't Stop No Show.*

Theatre credits includes: *The Fellowship, The Memory of Water, The Death of a Black Man* (Hampstead Theatre); *Overflow, Chiaroscuro, An Adventure, The Trick* [also tour] (Bush Theatre); *An unfinished man* (Yard Theatre); *Princess and the Hustler* (Bristol Old Vic / tour), *Black Men Walking* (Scottish tour); *Again* (West End); *Abigail's Party* (Hull Truck); *Black Men Walking* (Manchester Royal Exchange / tour); *Fences* (West End / Theatre Royal Bath); *A Raisin in the Sun* (Sheffield Crucible / tour); *Ticking* (West End); *Play Mas* (Orange Tree Theatre).

Film credits include: *Bluebird, Samuel's Trousers, Bruce, Gypsy's Kiss, The Knot, High Tide, What We Did On Our Holiday* (children), *Common People, Tezz, Final Prayer, Love / Loss, Stop, A Sunny Morning, Value Life, Conversation Piece, 10by10.*

Television credits include: *Outnumbered* (children); *Just Around the Corner* (children); *Dickensian* (children); *Inside the Mind of Leonardo.*

INGRID MACKINNON
MOVEMENT DIRECTOR

Ingrid Mackinnon is a London based movement director and choreographer.

For Kiln: *Girl on an Altar* – Movement & Intimacy Director.

Movement direction credits include: *Playboy of the West Indies* (Birmingham Rep); *The Meaning of Zong* (Bristol Old Vic / UK tour); *Moreno* (Theatre503); *Red Riding Hood* (Theatre Royal Stratford East); *Antigone* (Mercury Theatre); *Romeo and Juliet* (Regent's Park Open Air Theatre – winner Black British Theatre Awards 2021 Best Choreography); *Liminal – Le Gateau Chocolat* (King's Head Theatre); *Liar Heretic Thief* (Lyric Hammersmith); *Reimagining Cacophony* (Almeida Theatre); *First Encounters: The Merchant of Venice*, *Kingdom Come* (RSC); *Josephine* (Theatre Royal Bath); *Typical* (Soho Theatre); *#WeAreArrested* (Arcola Theatre and RSC); *The Border* (Theatre Centre); *Fantastic Mr. Fox* (as Associate Movement Director, Nuffield Southampton and National / International tour); *Hamlet*, *#DR@CULA!* (Royal Central School of Speech and Drama); *Bonnie and Clyde* (UWL: London College of Music).

Other credits include: Intimacy support for *101 Dalmatians, Legally Blonde, Carousel* (Regent's Park Open Air Theatre).

SAMANTHA E ADAMS
PRODUCTION DRAMATHERAPIST

Sam is an HCPC registered freelance Dramatherapist, consultant, visiting lecturer, and academic researcher. She was a performer for over two decades. Sam teaches the Therapeutic Stories Unit at the University of Roehampton on the Dramatherapy MA, where she trained. She also contributes annually to the Applied Theatre MA at the Royal Central School of Speech and Drama teaching the Pedagogy of Storytelling. Sam has led and facilitated the Health and Wellbeing Course to members of Clean Break Theatre Company since 2017 and has a small Therapy and Supervision private practice.

Dramatherapist credits include: *Trouble in Mind* (National Theatre).

Wellbeing Consultancy credits include: *Clynborne Park* (Park Theatre); *Long Covid Project* (The Old Vic); *Moreno* (Theatre503); *The Meaning of Zong* (Bristol Old Vic).

She is an Executive Member of the British Association of Dramatherapists where she recently proposed and facilitated the conference 'Carnival of Canboulay: Dialogues about Race & Power at play in Dramatherapy' and is co-editor of the Special Issue Dramatherapy Journal 'Necessary Voices and Narratives'.

Performance credits include: Master of Ceremonies (Royal Court Theatre's late-night cabaret); Take Up Space curated by Vishni Vela Billson (Royal Court) and Liselle Terret (UEL).

ELEANOR MANNERS
VOICE & DIALECT COACH

Voice credits include: *Jitney* (The Old Vic); *seven methods of killing kylie jenner*, *Is God Is* (Royal Court Theatre); *Othello* (National Youth Theatre); *Searching for the Heart of Leeds, Jitney, Wendy and Peter Pan* (Leeds Playhouse); *Klippies* (Young Vic Theatre); *Cake* (Theatre Peckham); *When this is Over* (Company Three); *Run it Back* (Talawa Theatre Company); *Love and Other Acts* (Donmar Warehouse); *White Noise* (Bridge Theatre); *White Card* (Northern Stage, national tour).

Directing credits include: *Jack Frost and the Search for Winter* (Tutti Frutti); *Wizard of Oz* (Leeds Playhouse).

MEGAN KEEGAN-PILMOOR
COSTUME SUPERVISOR

Megan trained at London College of Fashion, and is a Costume Supervisor and Wardrobe Manager working predominately in London, including the West End.

For Kiln: *Black Love, The Invisible Hand, Reasons You Should(n't) Love Me, Pass Over, Blues in the Night, The Son* (also West End).

Theatre credits include: *Pride and Prejudice* (*sort of)* (West End); *Once*

Upon a Time in Nazi Occupied Tunisia, Ink, Twilight Zone (Almeida Theatre); Sweet Charity, Measure for Measure, The Resistible Rise of Arturo Ui, The Shakespeare Trilogy, Les Liaisons Dangereuses (Donmar Warehouse); Circus 1903 (Royal Festival Hall, Southbank Centre); Long Day's Journey into Night (West End / Brooklyn Academy of Music, New York / The Wallis Center for Performing Arts, LA); Follies (National Theatre); Heisenberg: The Uncertainty Principle (West End); Julius Caesar, Antony and Cleopatra (Royal Shakespeare Company).

Opera credits include: Otello (Grange Park Opera).

KEISHA BANYA
WIGS SUPERVISOR

Keisha Banya is a London based hair and makeup artist; she graduated from West Thames specialist hair and makeup course in 2019.

Theatre credits include: A Doll's House, Part 2 (Donmar Warehouse); A Number [Olivier Award nomination], Camp Siegfried (The Old Vic); The Two-Character Play (Hampstead Theatre).

She also works alongside institutions such as RADA, LAMDA and RAM to provide industry-standard lessons and hair and makeup support for final year shows.

KATE WATERS
FIGHT DIRECTOR

Theatre credits include: Regular work at the National Theatre, RSC, Donmar Warehouse, Shakespeare's Globe and in the West End. She has also worked in many of the country's regional theatres. Recent work includes Macbeth (Almeida Theatre); Small Island (National Theatre); Henry V (Donmar Warehouse); Cyrano de Bergerac (West End, Glasgow & Brooklyn); Tina, The Musical (West End & Germany); Sweat (Donmar Warehouse & West End).

Television credits include: Coronation Street, Emmerdale and Hollyoaks on all of which she is a regular fight director.

Film credits include: My Policeman (Amazon Studios); Death of England (Sky Arts & National Theatre – BAFTA Nominee for Best Single Drama); Romeo and Juilet (Sky Arts, PBS America & National Theatre); Gym (RADA, Short Film); Pondlife, Making Noises Quietly (Open Palm Films).

She is also a qualified boxing coach and coaches at Rathbone Amateur Boxing Club.

STEPHEN BAILEY
ASSISTANT DIRECTOR

Stephen trained at LAMDA. Their work foregrounds disabled and neurodivergent presences in existing stories.

Directing credits include: SURFACING (in development); Who Plays Who (The Barbican); How to Make a Cup of Tea (Graeae); Little Echoes (The Hope); Access Platform (VAULT Festival); Invisible Condition (Camden Etcetera); The Dark Things (LAMDA) and the short film Yoga for the Feet.

Assisting credits include: Our Generation (National Theatre / Chichester Festival Theatre); Witness for the Prosecution (West End); One Under (Graeae); Andre Chenier (Royal Opera House); The Cost of Living (Hampstead Theatre); The Crucible (Weöres Sándor Színház); Returning to Haifa (Finborough).

They are a two-time finalist for the Young Vic Theatre Genesis Future Director's Award. Previously they were Resident Assistant Director for Chichester Festival Theatre and the European Theatre Convention. Stephen is the Artistic Director of ASYLUM Arts an arts advocacy organisation focused on developing and empowering neurodivergent talent. ASYLUM Arts are a resident company on the Barbican Lab Scheme supported by Arts Council England.

K_{THEATRE} L N

"Kiln Theatre has revitalised the cultural life of Brent and brings world-class theatre at an affordable price to people from all walks of life."
Zadie Smith

Kiln Theatre sits in the heart of Kilburn in Brent, a unique and culturally diverse area of London where over 140 languages are spoken. We are a newly refurbished, welcoming and proudly local venue, with an internationally acclaimed programme of world and UK premieres. Our work presents the world through a variety of lenses, amplifying unheard / ignored voices into the mainstream, exploring and examining the threads of human connection that cross race, culture and identity.

"This place was a special cocoon. Now she has grown and blossomed into a beautiful butterfly." **Sharon D Clarke**

We believe that theatre is for all and want everyone to feel welcome and entitled to call the Kiln their own. We are committed to nurturing the talent of young people and providing a platform for their voices to be heard.

"I wanted to say thank you for creating the most diverse theatre I have been to. In terms of race, culture, class, age, everything – not only in the selection of shows and actors, but in the audience."
Audience member, 2021

We look forward to welcoming you to Kilburn.

Kiln Theatre
269 Kilburn High Road,
London, NW6 7JR

KilnTheatre.com

info@KilnTheatre.com

 @KilnTheatre

Registration No. 1396429. Charity No. 276892

FOR KILN THEATRE

THANK YOU

We are so grateful to all our supporters, whose donations enable us to use the power of storytelling to champion unheard voices and to ensure that everyone can experience the power of theatre.

STATUTORY FUNDERS

Arts Council England

MAJOR DONORS AND KILN CIRCLE

Primrose and David Bell

Jules and Cheryl Burns

Sir Trevor and Lady Susan Chinn

Matthew Greenburgh and Helen Payne

Ros and Alan Haigh

Jonathan Levy and Gabrielle Rifkind

Adam Kenwright

Frances Magee

Lady Susie Sainsbury

Jon and NoraLee Sedmak

Christopher Yu

INDIVIDUALS

Penny Badowska

James Baer and Henry Chu

Laure Duvoisin

Carol and Gary Fethke

Sue Fletcher

Betise Head

Nicola Horton and Tiffany Evans

Atalanta Goulandris

Alan Maclean and Jo Corkish

Elaine Morris

Richard Naylor

Sarah and Joseph Zarfaty

TRUSTS AND FOUNDATIONS

29th May 1961 Charitable Trust

The Austin and Hope Pilkington Trust

Backstage Trust

BBC Children in Need

Bertha Foundation

Boris Karloff Charitable Foundation

Chapman Charitable Trust

City Bridge Trust

The D'Oyly Carte Charitable Trust

Esmée Fairbairn Foundation

Foyle Foundation

Garfield Weston Foundation

The Golsoncott Foundation

John Lyon's Charity

The John Thaw Foundation

Marie-Louise von Motesiczky Charitable Trust

Pears Foundation

The Roddick Foundation

The Royal Victoria Hall Foundation

Stanley Thomas Johnson Foundation

Three Monkies Trust

Wellington Management UK Foundation

The Vanderbilt Family Foundation

Young Londoners Fund

COMPANIES

Bloomberg Philanthropies

Doorstep Puppet Theatre

Synergy Vision

We are grateful to Arts Council England, DCMS and HM Treasury for our grant from the Culture Recovery Fund.

Supported using public funding by
ARTS COUNCIL ENGLAND
LOTTERY FUNDED

HERE FOR CULTURE

HM Government

WE ARE GRATEFUL FOR THE SUPPORT OF THIS PRODUCTION FROM:

Bertha Foundation fights for a more just world. They support activists, storytellers, and lawyers who are working to bring about social and economic justice and human rights for all.

The Golsoncott Foundation

The Royal Victoria Hall Foundation

Access All Areas make disruptive theatre and performance by learning disabled and autistic artists.

Our performances create intimate moments of interaction between performers and public, occupying unexpected spaces in venues, on the streets and in public buildings.

We also train and consult theatre, film, and TV companies in how to be more accessible throughout their creative practice, from Front-of-House, to communications, to castings, to rehearsals and on-set work. By working with wonderful partners like Kiln Theatre, we create more space for learning disabled and autistic artists, co§mmunities, and audiences in the arts.

If you think our access consultancy might be useful for your organisation, or want to find out more about our work, go to **accessallareastheatre.org/consultancy/** or email **hello@accessallareastheatre.org**.

 Supported using public funding by
ARTS COUNCIL ENGLAND

The Darkest Part of the Night

For MaKhupe and Noma

Characters

Dwight, *early 50s in the present day. He is an autistic person who speaks with a Yorkshire accent | also plays 11-year-old version of himself in 1981.*

Shirley, **Dwight**'s *older sister, early 50s in the present day. She speaks with a Yorkshire accent | same actor also plays* **Josephine**, **Shirley** *and* **Dwight**'s *mother, early 40s in 1981. She speaks with a hybrid Yorkshire/Jamaican accent. At times she interweaves English with patois.*

Calvin, **Shirley**'s *husband, early 50s in the present day. Speaks with a Yorkshire accent | same actor also plays* **Leroy**, **Shirley** *and* **Dwight**'s *father. Mid-40s in 1981. He speaks with a hybrid Yorkshire/Jamaican accent. At times he interweaves English with patois.*

Young Shirley, **Dwight**'s *sister, 13 years old in 1981. Speaks with a Yorkshire accent.*

Anna, **Dwight**'s *social worker in 1981. Mid-20s, speaks with a London accent |* **Voices on the Radio**

Mr Campbell, **Dwight** *and* **Young Shirley**'s *Deputy Headteacher in 1981 | same actor also plays* **Police Officer** *and* **Prison Officer** *in 1981 |* **Voices on the Radio**

Set in Leeds in the present day and between June–August 1981.

Notes

/ indicates overlapping dialogue.

Stage directions relating to Dwight give instruction to the neurodivergent performer on actions, and further context to emotions and form.

Throughout the play Dwight stims in response to various emotions. Stimming actions vary in intensity. The type of stimming actions are open for the actor to explore.

Act One

Scene One

The Williams' House, *present day*

On stage there's a dining table with a lace cloth, flowers, four chairs and a handbag. **Dwight** *enters wearing a white shirt, a small suit jacket and a pair of jeans. He's carrying his trainers. He notices his mother's handbag. It unsettles him. He drops the trainers on the floor. He paces at first, then repeatedly exits and enters the room.*

When he chooses to stay, he reaches out to touch the bag, but recoils each time. He suddenly grabs the bag, looks inside and pours out the contents. He sits, holding the bag close to his face and smells it. Beat.

Shirley *enters from the kitchen. She's wearing a black dress and carries a hairbrush.* **Dwight** *turns away from her and hides the bag behind his back. She notices her belongings on the floor. Beat. She kisses her teeth and tosses the brush on the table. She starts picking up the items. She reaches in between his legs.* **Dwight** *doesn't move.*

While on the floor **Shirley** *sees the handbag behind his back. She reaches for it, but* **Dwight** *snatches it first.* **Shirley** *gets up and places her belongings on the table. She starts brushing* **Dwight**'s *hair without asking. Her strokes are fast and rough.* **Dwight** *uses the bag to cover his head.*

Shirley   Fine. You do it.

Shirley *holds out the brush. He doesn't take it.*

Young Shirley *enters dressed in a school uniform. She's carrying* **Dwight**'s *backpack. She stops when she sees him hiding. This is* **Dwight**'s *memory from 1981.*

Young Shirley (*to* **Dwight**)   What are you doing?

Dwight *lowers his arms at the sound of* **Young Shirley**'s *voice. He looks to* **Shirley** *to check if she sees* **Young Shirley**. *She doesn't.*

Shirley   Take it then.

He looks back at **Young Shirley**.

Dwight   Shirley?

Young Shirley *and* **Shirley** (*together*)   Yeah.

Dwight *pulls the handbag back down over his face.*

Young Shirley   C'mon, Dwight,

Shirley   We're going to be late.

Shirley *places the brush down and gathers her belongings.* **Young Shirley** *approaches him. She sits on the floor in front of him and undoes his laces.*

Young Shirley   Mum better not catch you with her bag again.

Shirley (*referring to the bag*)   Can I please use it?

Dwight *holds it tighter.* **Shirley** *gives up and exits.* **Dwight** *watches her leave.*

Young Shirley   Keep your foot straight. (*He turns back.*) We've got to leg it to school today. Rachel wants to take the backseat on the coach. Me and Calvin called dibs at break yesterday. I swear she's always trying to copy me. (*She pulls him up and takes the handbag away from him.*) Here. (*Hands him his backpack. He puts it on.*) Let me see your hair. (*He bends down to show her.*) You know how to do it. Just like mum showed you. (*She hands him the brush.*) I'm getting my suitcase. Five minutes and then we're out.

Young Shirley *exits. Beat.* **Dwight** *strokes the bristles with his finger. He glides the brush across his palm. He does this a few times before he brushes his hair. His strokes are slow and gentle. The sensation makes him smile.*

The doorbell rings. **Young Shirley** *enters.*

Young Shirley   Calvin's here.

Shirley *enters.*

Shirley (*calls out*)   Car's here, Calvin. (*To* **Dwight**.) C'mon.

The doorbell rings. He doesn't move. **Young Shirley** *takes his hand and pulls him towards her.*

Young Shirley   C'mon, I'm going to miss the coach.

The doorbell rings again. The noise bothers him. His stimming continues.

Shirley   We're going out the back door.

Young Shirley *pulls him forward.*

Young Shirley   Stop messing about.

Dwight *pulls against* **Shirley** *and* **Young Shirley**. *He's getting frustrated. He starts stimming.*

Shirley   You don't need your school bag today.

Young Shirley   Don't take your bag off, D.

The doorbell rings again. The noise bothers him. His stimming starts to intensify.

Shirley (*to* **Dwight**)   We talked about this.

Young Shirley (*yells out*)   Mum?

Dwight (*yells out*)   Mum!

Young Shirley (*yells out*)   He won't come. (*Beat.*) Mum?!

Young Shirley *exits.* **Dwight** *feels overwhelmed by the demands from* **Young Shirley** *and* **Shirley**. **Shirley** *steps away. It's been a while since she's seen her brother display such distressed behaviour.*

Dwight   Mum! Mum! Mum! Mum!

He continues as **Calvin** *enters dressed in a suit.*

Calvin   What's happened?

Shirley (*watching* **Dwight**)   The doorbell set him off.

Beat.

Calvin   Are you sure that you want him to go?

Shirley   He has to. Where are the programmes?

Calvin   Thought you had them.

Shirley   I must have left them upstairs.

Calvin   Are you okay?

Shirley   I'm fine. Just get him in the car.

Shirley *exits. Beat.* **Calvin** *steps closer to him.*

Calvin   Big man, remember what we said is happening
today.

He tries to touch **Dwight**. **Dwight** *reacts by shoving* **Calvin** *to the
ground. Lights down on the dining room.* **Dwight** *continues
stimming. Beat. 'My God is Real' by Mahalia Jackson starts to play.*
Dwight *recognises the tune. He hums the melody. It starts to calm
him.*

Dwight   'My God is Real'. Mahalia Jackson. 1963. Written
by Sallie Martin and Kenneth Morris in 1944.

Shirley *enters carrying a wreath of flowers reading, 'MUM' and
'JOSIE'.* **Dwight** *continues singing.* **Calvin** *stands.* **Shirley** *places
the flowers down.* **Dwight** *notices them. He stops pacing and
watches them for a moment. Suddenly, he charges down stage, where
the casket would be. There's an audible gasp.* **Dwight** *stops shy of
touching the casket. Beat.*

Calvin *and* **Shirley** *watch* **Dwight**'s *hand reach out to touch the
flowers. He recoils. He repeats this action a few times. It unsettles
him. He continues singing 'My God is Real' to himself. Three chairs
appear in a row away behind* **Dwight**. **Shirley** *sits.* **Calvin** *stands
beside her. Silence.*

Scene Two

Church of God of Prophecy, *present day*

Calvin *and* **Shirley** *watch* **Dwight**.

Calvin (*turns to* **Shirley**)   Some of the elders can't keep standing around any much longer. They thought we'd be halfway through the burial by now.

Shirley   Offer them lifts home.

Calvin   They don't think it's right to leave without seeing your mum being laid to rest.

Shirley   Guess they'll have to keep waiting then.

Calvin *sits.*

Calvin   That's your family Shirley /

Shirley (*shakes her head*)   Those are Leroy's chatty mouth people. /

Calvin   Your dad's people are your people.

Shirley   Mummy's side knows how to behave. They don't turn every situation into the Real Housewives of Leeds.

Young Shirley's voice (*softly to* **Dwight**) Hey, D.

Dwight *stops singing and looks around for* **Young Shirley**. **Dwight** *is caught between scattered memories and voices; and the grief of the present day.*

Calvin   They were all just a little shocked by Dwight's reaction, that's all.

Shirley   He didn't ram into the coffin and send her body flying into the air like some express delivery to God.

Calvin   They're not around enough to know what he's like.

Shirley (*scoffs*)   And whose fault is that? They've had plenty of chances.

Young Shirley *runs in.*

Young Shirley   Over here!

Young Shirley's voice (*softly*)   Over here.

Dwight *looks around for* **Young Shirley** *again.* **Young Shirley** *laughs and hides behind* **Shirley** *and* **Calvin**. *They don't see* **Young Shirley** *or* **Dwight**'s *interactions with her.*

Dwight (*sees* **Young Shirley**)   Shirley, stop hiding?

Shirley (*to* **Dwight**)   D, do you remember any of them ever coming over to give mum a break or to spend time with you? (*Beat.* **Dwight** *doesn't answer.*) Are you still not talking to me? /

Young Shirley   What are you still doing here?

Dwight (*to* **Young Shirley**)   I don't want to go without Mum.

Calvin *approaches* **Shirley** *and hugs her.* **Dwight** *approaches* **Young Shirley**.

Calvin   You both did her proud. It was a beautiful service

Young Shirley (*to* **Dwight**)   Do you remember why she said we had to start going to school by ourselves?

Shirley   He wants her more than me.

Calvin   It's not true.

Shirley   They did everything together.

Calvin   I get that, but he has to let us bury her now. It's been over half an hour.

Shirley   I know how long it's been, Cal.

Young Shirley (*to* **Dwight**)   She said that we were grown up and we didn't need her anymore.

Dwight *steps away from* **Young Shirley**.

Dwight (*to the audience*)   No!

Shirley (*to* **Calvin**)   Just stop pushing, you're upsetting him.

Calvin (*to* **Dwight**)   D, it's starting to rain at the cemetery.

Shirley   Then go back outside and tell everyone to go home.

Dwight *shows signs that he's about to start stimming.* **Young Shirley** *approaches him.*

Young Shirley (*to* **Dwight**)   Use your words. Tell me what's upsetting you? (*Beat.* **Dwight** *looks at* **Shirley** *and* **Calvin**.) When they get loud, you need to get louder.

Dwight   You don't listen to me anymore.

Young Shirley (*to* **Dwight**)   Try it. Try it now. (*Calls out.*) Say Shirley, Calvin, I have a voice too.

Shirley   We don't know what's going on in his head right now. Maybe he's mad at us for not letting him go to the hospital every day. Maybe he thinks we didn't check on them enough. I'm the eldest. It's my responsibility.

Calvin   She didn't tell anyone she was sick.

Shirley (*to* **Calvin**)   I should have noticed that she wasn't eating properly. I should have sent her straight to the GP and we'd have known her cancer was back.

Calvin   You know what our parents were like. Their limbs will be falling off, but they'll still say they don't want to make a fuss.

Shirley   I've been so caught up with the school becoming an academy –

Calvin   You're supposed to be on bereavement leave.

Shirley   I'm the headteacher, Cal. The school can't stop emailing me. But I can see that Dwight hasn't slept in three weeks. We've got a lot going on, Cal.

Calvin   Those boys need someone.

Shirley   Family is more important.

Dwight (*to* **Young Shirley**)   I want to go back, Shirley. I want Mum to walk us to school like when we were little. I don't want to be here. Make it all go back.

Beat. **Calvin** *and* **Shirley** *look at* **Dwight**.

Shirley   I think we should stay at Mum's for good.

There's a silence between **Calvin** *and* **Shirley**.

Young Shirley (*to* **Dwight**)   We can't go back.

Dwight *starts stimming.*

Calvin   We'll get more carers.

Dwight (*yells out*)   Don't say that!

Shirley (*to* **Dwight**)   I wouldn't do that to you, D.

Calvin   Maxine said she can look for funding to get him some respite days.

Shirley   When did you speak to his social worker? Have you two come up with a care plan behind my back? (*To* **Dwight**.) Calm down. (*To* **Calvin**.) We're not white people, Calvin! We don't just throw our family into those care homes and forget about them. What if they don't cream his skin and brush his hair?

Dwight (*to himself*)   Dwight lives at home with Mummy, Daddy and Shirley.

Young Shirley (*to* **Dwight**)   You don't just stay at home. We go outside too. There are bad places and people out there. What are you going to do if you can't take care of yourself?

Dwight (*to himself*)   Stop talking to me. I want happy memories. Only happy memories of us.

Young Shirley *pulls* **Dwight** *to play Adventure Game.* **Calvin** *and* **Shirley** *don't acknowledge what's happening around them.* **Dwight** *is pulled into his memories.*

Calvin   You act like you're the only one that knows what's best for him. Don't forget I've known you since we were kids.

Beat. **Shirley** *exits. Lights down on the church.* **Young Shirley** *and* **Dwight** *continue playing.* **Calvin** *exits.* **Mr Campbell** *enters carrying a school bell. He watches them.* **Mr Campbell** *rings the bell. The ringing interrupts* **Dwight**'s *joyous memory of play.*

The memories will collide and be interrupted often. **Dwight** *will be pulled back and forth between the past and present as he tries to navigate his grief and relationships.*

Scene Three

Bexley Middle School, *June 1981*

There's a soundscape of children in the hall.

Dwight   We need to save the crystals or the Argonds will trap us on their planet.

Young Shirley   The first bell's gone. You have to go to class, D.

Dwight (*hops*)   Green, triangle, square, blue, triangle. Go!

Young Shirley   I have to go on my trip.

Dwight   I don't want you to go too. Stay with me.

Mr Campbell   You're going to make your sister miss the coach, lad.

Young Shirley   Sorry, D.

She turns to leave. **Dwight** *tries to follow her.* **Mr Campbell** *blocks his path.*

Mr Campbell   Year 7s don't get to go on school trips yet.

Dwight   I can camp too.

Young Shirley   As if! You love your bed too much. Two sleeps then I'm back.

Mr Campbell (*to* **Dwight**)   Don't you have your own friends to play with?

Young Shirley   No one will play with him, sir. They don't like that he lines up the footballs instead of kicking them. (*To* **Dwight**.) Naureen didn't mind.

Mr Campbell   What class is she in?

Young Shirley   They used to go to the same primary together. But she goes to the grammar school now. Her dad says it's the best school.

Mr Campbell   Well, Bexley Middle School has a new deputy head teacher and I'm going to make this a beacon school.

Young Shirley   Mrs Harris was an excellent teacher. I wish she didn't have to go.

Dwight   I liked Mrs Harris.

Mr Campbell   Teachers retire.

Young Shirley   Maybe if you let Jamal come back, we'll start liking you too.

Mr Campbell   Jamal was a troublemaker.

Young Shirley   He made a stink bomb in science, that's well smart.

Mr Campbell   I had to call the fire department and ambulances.

Young Shirley   Everyone was taking the piss and coughing to get out of doing the exam.

Mr Campbell   Disruptive behaviour will no longer be tolerated.

Young Shirley   He said sorry.

Mr Campbell   Rules and policies are being strictly enforced from now on. (*He approaches* **Dwight**.) Those jeans are not school uniform.

Dwight *scratches and shrugs as if recalling an itching sensation.*

Dwight   Trousers scratch my skin.

Mr Campbell   Trousers are school uniform. Your mum knows this.

Young Shirley   She tried to get him new ones but he screamed down Woolworths last weekend. He took them off right there on the shop floor. She had to pinch his ears and dragged him back to the changing rooms.

Dwight *steps out of the memory for a moment.* **Mr Campbell** *and* **Young Shirley** *don't hear him.*

Dwight   Don't tell him anything about us, Shirley. He doesn't like me.

Young Shirley   The security guard wanted to throw us out. I swear he thought he was sixteen cos of how big he looks.

Dwight   I'm eleven.

Mr Campbell (*to* **Dwight**)   Causing problems everywhere you go.

Dwight   I'm not a problem.

Young Shirley   Mum says he's different.

Dwight   I'm different.

Mr Campbell   Right double team you two are. You must be a handful for her.

Young Shirley (*to* **Mr Campbell**)   I help around the house a lot actually. I do all the cooking for us when she's on nights at the infirmary.

Mr Campbell   She leaves you two alone?

Young Shirley   I'm not a baby. I'm thirteen.

Mr Campbell   Yes, but messing with the cooker is dangerous.

Young Shirley   I'm a better chef than Delia Smith. (*To* **Dwight**.) Tell him what I put in your crisp butty.

Dwight   Cheese, salt and vinegar crisps and hot pepper sauce.

Young Shirley   The chef's special.

Mr Campbell   That's not a proper dinner. Your mum should feed you properly.

Dwight   Mum's food is delicious.

Young Shirley   But Dad can't cook.

Mr Campbell   Your dad's around?

Young Shirley   Of course, why wouldn't he be?

Dwight   Dwight lives at home with Mummy, Daddy and Shirley.

Mr Campbell   You know one day Shirley is going to leave you and go off to the polytechnic or a university out of Leeds.

Young Shirley   I'm not going to university. I'm going to be an explorer. Go off to Africa and the North Pole instead.

Mr Campbell (*to* **Young Shirley**)   How about you just stay in your own class first, instead of wandering off to mouth off at Dwight's teachers.

Young Shirley   I wouldn't have to if Miss Clephan didn't pick on him.

Mr Campbell   Teachers don't pick on students.

Dwight   They put pencils in my hair.

Mr Campbell   The teachers?

Young Shirley   Boys in his class.

Dwight   All the boys are mean.

Young Shirley   Except Calvin. He's nice. You're only allowed to play with Calvin. But today you'll have to find someone to eat lunch with. (*To* **Mr Campbell**.) He used to eat lunch with Mrs Harris and she'd also help him with his work. She should have been the next deputy head.

Mr Campbell   Well, if you graduate from university, you can come back and be the deputy head one day.

Young Shirley   I'd rather smell Dwight's farts for the rest of my life than be a teacher here.

Mr Campbell   That's a shame. You have great potential, Shirley.

Young Shirley   A shame is staying in school when I don't have to. (*She turns to leave.*) I'm off, D. Wait up for yeah.

She exits. **Dwight** *tries to follow her.* **Mr Campbell** *blocks his path. There's a stand-off. Beat.* **Dwight** *steps to the side.* **Mr Campbell** *mimics him. They repeat this action twice more.*

Mr Campbell   And what are you going to be on day? (*Beat.*) I hope not a pain in my side. (**Dwight** *feels scared and humiliated. He starts stimming. The intensity is low but noticeable to* **Mr Campbell**.) I hear your name a lot in the staff room. They say you disrupt a lot of your lessons. I don't want trouble from you while Shirley's away.

Mr Campbell *checks his watch. It's time for the second bell. He rings the bell and stops. It unsettles* **Dwight**. *His stimming grows slightly. He hums Stevie Wonder's 'I Ain't Going to Stand For It' to calm himself. Beat.*

Mr Campbell   That's the second bell. You're late for class. Detention. (*Beat.*) Follow me.

Mr Campbell *exits.* **Dwight** *continues stimming and humming the song.*

Dwight (*to himself*)   Use your words, D. (*He wants to calm down but still feels upset.*) Mr Campbell is a bully. Bullies are mean. Bullying is bad. I don't like it. I don't like him.

He hums the song louder. Lights up on a record player on stage. The record player sits on top of a small cabinet. Behind sliding glass doors are vinyl records.

Scene Four

The Williams' House, *June 1981*

Dwight *rushes to the cabinet. Simultaneously,* **Leroy** *enters wearing blue overalls and a jacket. He heads to the cabinet too. He's stopped by* **Dwight** *tossing his backpack and jacket on the floor.*

Dwight *kicks off his shoes in the direction of the cabinet. He opens the cabinet and searches for the song he's been humming all day. He doesn't take notice of* **Leroy***.*

Leroy   If you break something, you'd better have money to pay for it.

Dwight *doesn't respond to him.* **Leroy** *kisses his teeth and picks up* **Dwight***'s belongings. He tosses them to the side.* **Leroy** *reaches over* **Dwight** *and opens the drinks cabinet.*

Leroy   This house doesn't come for free you know. (*He pours himself a Bell's whisky and downs it.* **Dwight** *watches him refill the glass. Beat.*) What? (*Beat.*) You want one? (**Dwight** *looks away.*) You roll your eyes like your mother. (*He sips his drink.*) Wait till you've got to put sugar in your teeth to make a rasclart manager smile when you'd rather box him in his head. (**Dwight** *picks a record.*) Show me what you've picked. (**Dwight** *knocks* **Leroy***'s drink when he stands.*) Watch what you are doing! (**Dwight** *flinches, drops the record, and backs away from* **Leroy***.*) Don't start with your hollaring. Mi neva touch yuh.

Josephine *enters wearing her nurse's uniform.*

Josephine   What's all the yelling for?

Dwight *runs to hug* **Josephine***.*

Leroy   He knocked my glass wid fi him big self.

Josephine   I'm sure you didn't do it on purpose. Daddy is sorry.

Leroy   Mi nuh sorry. He spilt my drink.

Josephine (*to* **Dwight**)   It's okay. Go play your music.

Leroy (*to* **Dwight**)   Aren't you going to say sorry to me?

Dwight *ignores* **Leroy***.*

Leroy   I don't like how he ignores me.

Josephine   You just shout at him too much.

Leroy   My father yelled, and I always listened.

Josephine   He drank alone too much to. You don't need to copy everything.

Beat.

Leroy   Yuh mek di bowy nuh respect mi, wen yuh chat tuh mi like dat.

Dwight *plays the record, Stevie Wonder's 'I Ain't Going to Stand For It'. He tries to put the headphones on* **Josephine**. *She's distracted with speaking to* **Leroy**.

Josephine   What are you even doing here, Leroy?

Leroy   Don't I live here?

Josephine   You're home early. Did you quarrel with your manager again?

Leroy (*refills his glass*)   No.

Josephine   Good. I can't have you losing any more hours. These split shifts are killing my feet.

Leroy   He fired me this time.

Beat. **Dwight** *pushing* **Josephine** *to the record playing. She maintains her gaze on* **Leroy**. **Dwight** *tries to put the headphones onto* **Josephine**. *She swipes them away.*

Josephine   You lost your job? /

Leroy   I didn't lose it. /

Dwight (*pulls* **Josephine**)   Mum, come and listen.

Leroy (*snaps*)   Dwight, can't you see I'm talking to your mother?!

Beat.

Josephine   What happened, Leroy?

Leroy   He fired the whole shop floor.

Josephine   Just like that?

Leroy   One hundred and twenty-five men just like that. No warning.

Dwight *pulls the jack out of the sound system. The music fills the room.* **Dwight** *moves the needle back to the start of the chorus and turns up the volume. He sings along to the record.*

Josephine *turns the music down.*

Leroy   The director came up from London last week. We knew something was happening. He never comes.

Josephine   You never said anything.

Leroy   The manager said he was only coming to reassure us that Lyons Manufactures wasn't going under like the other factories up in Sheffield. He said, as long as this is England, families would still need boilers to heat up their homes. Then this morning we get there, and it's all locked up and the receivers are coming tomorrow.

Josephine   So quick?

Dwight *turns the music back up.*

Leroy (*kisses his teeth*)   Lying rasshole! We're in a recession but the director's Mercedes looks shiny like it just came off the lot.

Josephine   What's the union saying? /

Leroy   What can they say?

Josephine (*snaps*)   Dwight, turn that down. (*To* **Leroy**.) The union should be protecting your jobs.

Dwight *doesn't turn it down.* **Josephine** *puts the jack back in and headphones on* **Dwight**.

Leroy   Five hundred union members marched for jobs from Liverpool to London in May and Thatcher still refused to see them. Look at them, a month later, they're still scrambling trying to save themselves. They don't give a damn about black workers on a normal day, let alone during a recession. (**Dwight** *pulls out the jack*. **Leroy** *clips him round the ear and turns the music off. To* **Dwight**.) Touch it again and I'll fetch my belt.

There's a moment of silence. **Dwight** *covers his ear.* **Josephine** *watches* **Dwight** *and* **Leroy***'s movements.* **Leroy** *refills his drink and sits. Beat.* **Josephine** *puts headphones back on* **Dwight** *and turn the music on. She approaches* **Leroy***, sits on his lap and takes his glass. She sips it.* **Dwight** *watches his parents. Beat.*

Josephine   So what are you going to do?

Leroy   I don't know, Josie. It just happened.

Beat.

Josephine   I'm sorry.

Beat.

Leroy   Twenty-five years I've been mashing up my ears on the loud presses and they boot me out like some old stinking cat.

Dwight *yanks out the jack and throws the headphones. The volume is loud.* **Leroy** *jumps to clip him again.* **Josephine** *pulls him back.* **Leroy** *sits.*

Josephine   Shouting just makes things worse. He needs to settle before I go.

Josephine *picks up the headphones and puts them back onto* **Dwight***. She turns down the volume.* **Leroy** *watches.* **Dwight** *claims* **Josephine** *by hugging her tightly.*

Leroy   What's his problem anyway?

Josephine   He misses Shirley.

Leroy   She's only gone until the weekend.

Josephine   Dwight and Shirley actually like each other, unlike you and your sister.

Leroy   I like Marcia just fine, but she is not one of the boys. Dwight needs play outside with his own friends.

Josephine   The neighbourhood is too rough for him.

Leroy   Saint Thomas toughened me and Samson.

Josephine   Samson was a quiet church boy back home. You and Curtis that roped him into bad situations when we got here.

Leroy   Everyone likes to think he is the righteous community barber, but me and Curtis know the truth. Samson got his hands dirty plenty of times to get that shop's deposit. We always had his back and because of us he has something to pass down to Calvin. Meanwhile the rest of us have nothing to show for working for somebody else most of our lives.

Leroy *sighs.* **Josephine** *wants to comfort* **Leroy** *but* **Dwight** *holds her back.*

Josephine   I can put him to bed early and we can keep talking before I go.

Leroy   What's left to say? It is what it is.

Beat.

Josephine   What do you need?

Leroy *looks at* **Dwight**.

Leroy   It's fine.

Josephine   That new comedy show, Three of a Kind is on tonight. Maybe you and Dwight can watch it. (*To* **Dwight**.) You could both use a good laugh.

Dwight *pushes her away.* **Leroy** *tuts.*

Leroy   Lenny Henry is not that funny.

Josephine   Just sey yuh jealous of him an keep it moving

Leroy   Real laughing is not the same as TV laughing. Let Lenny come in front of my face and tell a joke.

Josephine   He doesn't need to be funny when he's that good looking.

Leroy   Ha! Now mi kno yuh lying.

Josephine   I said what I said.

Leroy *slowly approaches* **Josephine**.

Leroy   Yuh si me? Yuh si di way mi luk. (*He slowly approaches her.*) Yuh si di way mi waak. Yuh si di way mi chat tuh. Yeah, dat baby, dat is real nice.

They're standing intimately close.

Josephine (*laughs*)   I see you, Leroy Williams.

Leroy   Aint nothing fake about us, Josephine Williams.

Josephine   Get changed. I'll heat you up some dinner.

Beat.

Leroy   No need. I'm popping out quickly.

Josephine   To go where?

Leroy   To see Curtis by Hayfield's.

Josephine   My second shift starts at 8pm.

Leroy   I won't be long.

Josephine   Don't you think you've had enough to drink already?

Leroy   I'm not going to the pub for a drink. Curtis said he can sort me out with some work.

Josephine   Ask Samson for work. /

Leroy   No /

Josephine   I'll ask him for you. /

Leroy I'm not working in the barber shop.

Josephine Why not? You spend all your time there anyway.

Leroy I take things apart and put them back together. I've done that since I was Dwight's age. That's who I am, Josie.

Josephine At least go to the Citizens Advice Bureau before it closes. If they have nothing, then you can go to Curtis.

Leroy I already know there's nothing.

Josephine How do you know that?

Leroy Do you see the scaffolding popping up everywhere in Chapeltown? That's the city council. They have contracted their jobs to a company in Wetherby to come all the way across Leeds to fix up our houses. We've got plenty of young skilled black labourers in the neighbourhood with idle hands and frustrated minds. The council could give us fair pay and pride in fixing up our own community. But they'd rather see us overwhelm the bureau and fill up the dole queue; and just so that they can keep saying we're lazy. (*Beat.*) Curtis keeps food on the table, Rachel and her sisters clothed and Pauline's happy. He's a good man.

Josephine He had a baby on Pauline laas year wid dat faas bow legged gyal.

Leroy You chatty mouth people spread too many lies.

Josephine It's not a lie if the truth is walking around in Pampers looking like a spitting image of Rachel.

He turns to leave.

Leroy I won't be late.

Josephine Don't bring the police back into this house, Leroy. (*He stops and turns back.*) We all know Curtis is responsible for that ram-raid up in Burnley last week.

Leroy You didn't say no to the crate of colas I brought back though.

He smiles and exits. **Josephine** *turns to* **Dwight**.

Josephine   I can eat with you before I go. Take your things
upstairs and get changed. (*He doesn't move.*) Dwight? (*Beat.*)
You've been quiet since I picked you up from school. (*Beat.*)
What did we say about using your words more? I can't read
your mind. C'mon, we practised. (*Beat.*) There's so much
knowledge in that big head of yours, you just need to learn
how to express it so that your teachers know how smart you
are. Education is the passport to the world, and you, my son,
are going places. You are going to get a big fancy job, get
married to a lovely girl and have your own children.

He rushes to hug her.

Dwight   I don't want that. I want to stay here with you.

Josephine   We can't stop change from happening, but we
can try to prepare ourselves for it.

He buries his face into her clothes. Beat.

Dwight   You always smell like flowers.

Josephine   Estée Lauder. Your mother only does luxury,
remember that when you retire me and start buying me
designer handbags from Marks and Spencer. (*She pulls away
from* **Dwight** *and goes towards the record player.*) My little bottle
of perfume split in my handbag. I guess buying a new one
will have to wait now. I'll need the extra hours during the
day at the hospital, so no more excuses, you and Shirley
have to take yourselves to and from school. (*She searches for a
record.*) You see how it all makes sense now. I didn't know life
was coming at me fast, but my God knew something that I
didn't know. He spoke to me weeks ago and told me to teach
you the bus routes and schedules. (*She picks 'Cherry Oh Baby'
by Eric Donaldson.*) I am going to miss our dancing sessions
after school. Maybe you can teach your father a little one two
step.

Dwight   Dad can't dance like me.

Josephine   If you give him the right record he'll loosen up. Stevie is always fun. But it doesn't get him going like Desmond Dekker or Jimmy Cliff. Music speaks to our souls. (*She plays.*) You feel that?

Dwight   Jamaican Song Competition winner 1971.

Josephine   And the name of the singer?

Dwight   Eric Donaldson.

Dwight *starts dancing.*

Josephine   Keep that joy, D. (*They dance. She sings to him and ad libs in between lyrics.*) We don't wear frowns in this family. We accept each other gladly. (**Dwight** *sings alone.*) Go on, Dwight.

Josephine *smiles and watches him for a moment. She exits. He doesn't notice her leaving. The music and lights start to fade.* **Dwight** *continues singing and dancing alone in a spotlight. He realises* **Josephine** *is gone. He stops singing. Panic sets in. He searches for her.*

Dwight   Mum? (*He calls out.*) Mum? Mum?! Not again. (*He closes his eyes tight and opens them.*) Come back. (*He closes his eyes tight and opens them.*) Come back. Don't leave me alone. (*He's starts stimming out of anxiousness.*) C'mon Dwight think, only happy things, only happy things, only happy things.

Lights snap up. He's back in the living room again.

Scene Five

The Williams' House, *June, 1981*

Young Shirley *enters dressed in her school uniform.*

Young Shirley   So I was up first. Rachel was standing at the bottom looking up at me, laughing and showing teeth like a hyena. I was climbing a ladder. It weren't that funny.

(**Dwight** *rushes over to her and hugs her.*) Ew, what are you doing?

Beat.

Dwight   I miss us being like this.

Young Shirley   Put me down you weirdo and get your shoes on. (*Beat. He puts her down. He collects his shoes while* **Young Shirley** *picks up his bag and jacket. She checks if his books are inside.* **Dwight** *unties his laces.*) Now where was I? (*Beat.*) Oh yeah so, Chantel told me on the coach that Rachel was off with me because Calvin let me ride his new Chopper bike and didn't give her a go. Like as if it's my bike to be giving goes on? (*Kisses her teeth.*) So, I'm by the handle bit for the zipwire and the instructor is like go when you're ready. I swear, D, the tree was taller than a skyscraper. I could see all the way from here to London. Rachel was looking up at me saying, don't piss your pants, Shirley. I'll piss on that perm, if you keep running your mouth, that's what I told her.

Josephine *enters still wearing a nurse's uniform.*

Josephine   Are you telling that story again?

Young Shirley   It's not my fault he didn't wait up for me.

Josephine   You know he goes straight to bed after he eats.

Young Shirley   Not when it's just me and him.

Josephine   That's because you force him to stay up. (*To* **Dwight**.) Hurry up and tie those laces, or you'll miss the bus.

Young Shirley   Dwight likes staying up with me . . . (*To* **Dwight**.) Tell her you like staying up with me.

Dwight   I like staying up with me.

Josephine *laughs.*

Young Shirley (*to* **Dwight**)   Funny.

Josephine (*to* **Dwight**)   Has she told you the Superman bit?

Dwight   No.

Josephine (*mimicking* **Young Shirley** *to* **Dwight**)   And then I went flying like Superman.

Young Shirley   I don't even sound like that.

Josephine (*mimicking* **Young Shirley**)   I was proper scared.

Young Shirley (*to* **Dwight**)   I was. I farted proper loud. (**Dwight** *laughs*.) Thank God I was so high, no one heard me.

Josephine   I hope you were wearing clean underwear.

Young Shirley   Of course I was.

Josephine   You get your periods now. You've got to make sure you're always clean.

Dwight (*giggles to* **Young Shirley**)   You get your periods now.

Young Shirley *is embarrassed.*

Young Shirley   Oh my God. Why are you two being so weird? I don't even want to finish my story now.

Josephine   Well, I'm glad you did the zipwire even though you were scared. It makes you brave and shows you what you're capable of. Same to you, D. Be scared but breakthrough.

The doorbell rings. **Dwight** *is jolted out of this memory. He stands and looks worried.*

Josephine   Thought you said Calvin was at the doctor's this morning.

Young Shirley   That's what he told me.

Josephine *heads to the door.* **Dwight** *follows behind her.*

Dwight   Mum, don't go to the door. Come back and tie my laces.

Josephine   Shirley, help him before he trips over and hurts himself.

Josephine *exits.* **Young Shirley** *pulls* **Dwight** *back. He nervously watches the door.*

Young Shirley (*to* **Dwight**)   At night they gave us hot chocolate and KitKats. I didn't eat mine. I saved it for later cos I knew I'd be hungry. Lunch was some dry piece of unseasoned chicken. I saw Miss Sullivan struggle to swallow it too. She knows what seasoning tastes like. Rachel told me this one time that she saw her down by Dutch Pot during carnival whining her flat English behind all up on some Rasta man.

Dwight *steps out of the memory for a moment.* **Young Shirley** *doesn't hear him.*

Dwight (*looking at the door*)   Shirley, don't let her in.

Young Shirley   Dwight, you're not listening to my story.

Josephine *and* **Anna***, a social worker, enter.* **Josephine***'s mood has changed.*

Josephine (*to* **Young Shirley**)   Shirley, go wake your father.

Young Shirley   What's wrong?

Josephine   Go.

Young Shirley *and* **Anna** *exchange looks.*

Anna   Good morning, Shirley.

Young Shirley   Hi.

Young Shirley *exits.* **Josephine** *notices* **Dwight***'s untied laces. She rushes to tie them.* **Dwight** *watches* **Anna** *as she looks around the house.* **Anna** *finally meets* **Dwight***'s gaze.*

Anna   You must be Dwight.

He looks away. **Josephine** *stands in front of him as if shielding him.*

Josephine   Please wait for my husband to come down.

Anna *decides to sit.*

Anna   You have a lovely home.

Beat.

Josephine   Thank you.

Anna (*to* **Dwight**)   Are you ready for school?

Josephine   He's brushed his teeth and eaten if you want to make a note of that.

Anna   Like I said this is just a welfare check.

Josephine   I keep my children clean.

Anna   I'm not accusing you of anything.

Josephine   Someone must have for you to be here. Tell me who reported us?

Anna   You know I can't tell you that.

Josephine   They kids can't be late for school.

Anna   I'll be as quick as I can. (*Beat.*) What does your husband do for work?

Josephine   Why are you asking about my husband? Has someone said something about Leroy?

Anna   These are just general questions, Mrs Williams.

Leroy *enters. He's only wearing a pyjama trousers.* **Young Shirley** *lurks by the door.*

Leroy (*to* **Josephine**)   Who's this?

Anna *stands and holds out her hand.*

Anna   Anna.

Leroy (*to* **Josephine**)   Jehovah's Witness?

Josephine   Social Services.

Leroy   Waah di social want?

Anna *looks backs and forth between them.*

Josephine (*to* **Leroy**)   Shi thinks wi neglecting di pickney /

Leroy (*to* **Anna**)   Do they look neglected to you? /

Anna   Let's all sit down. (*Looks over to* **Young Shirley**.) Shirley, you can come in.

Shirley *enters.* **Leroy** *steps in front of* **Anna**. **Anna** *steps back.*

Leroy (*to* **Anna**)   Don't address my daughter.

Josephine   Shirley, take your brother and go to school.

Anna   Actually, I need to speak to Shirley alone /

Josephine *and* **Leroy** *look at* **Young Shirley**.

Young Shirley   I didn't do anything. Mum, I've not even been here. /

Leroy (*to* **Young Shirley**)   Don't talk back to your mother.

Dwight *goes to stand beside* **Young Shirley**. *He holds her hand.*

Anna (*to* **Young Shirley**)   It's okay. You're not in trouble. /

Leroy (*to* **Anna**)   You can't talk to my child alone. /

Anna   I must follow procedures. /

Leroy   I'm staying in the room or you're not talking to her. /

Josephine (*to* **Leroy**)   Leroy, she said she'd come back with the police if I didn't let her in to the house.

Leroy (*to* **Anna**)   What right do you have to bring the police into my house?

Anna   I have a referral.

Leroy   That damn piece of paper doesn't have jurisdiction in my house /

Anna   Please calm down /

Leroy   Don't tell me how to behave in my home!

Anna *feels threatened. Beat.*

Anna   Okay. (*Beat.*) I think it's best that I just see myself out.

Josephine (*under her breath*)   Leroy, I don't want police cars in front of my house for the neighbours to see. (*To* **Anna**.) We'll be in the kitchen. Dwight, let's go.

Anna   Dwight can stay too. (*Beat.* **Josephine** *is reluctant.* **Leroy** *leads her out. Beat.* **Young Shirley** *and* **Dwight** *remain standing*). You can sit down. I don't bite. I promise.

Dwight *leads them to the chairs.* **Anna** *takes out a notebook from her handbag.*

Young Shirley   What's that for?

Anna   It's for making notes.

Young Shirley   Notes about what?

Anna   When I come to meet families like yours I make notes so that I know how to help them.

Young Shirley   We don't need help.

Anna   Everyone needs help at some point. (*Beat.* **Anna** *gets settled with a pen in hand.*) So, why don't you tell me how you're doing this morning? Dwight?

Dwight   I'm fine.

Anna (*to* **Dwight**)   I see you're ready for school. Where is it?

Young Shirley   In Crossgates.

Anna (*to* **Dwight**)   And how do you get there?

Young Shirley   By bus.

Anna   Shirley, maybe Dwight can tell me how he gets to school. (*Beat.*) Dwight, tell me.

Dwight   Walk down Mexborough Grove to Chapeltown Road. Turn right at the laundrette. Press the button at the crossing and wait for the green man. Cross the street when its beeping and wait for the number 2 into town. 2p each for me and Shirley. 7p for Mum /

Young Shirley Mum lets us go on our own now.

Anna Right, okay. (**Anna** *makes a note.* **Young Shirley** *peers over to look at the notes.*) It's a big responsibility to go by yourselves.

Dwight Calvin comes with us.

Anna Who is Calvin?

Young Shirley He's my friend. He lives two streets up.

Anna *makes another note.*

Anna What's it like when you come back home after school? What do you two like doing together?

Dwight Tidying up.

Young Shirley (*to* **Dwight**) She asked what we like.

Anna Well, maybe Dwight likes tidying up.

Young Shirley He likes playing with Calvin, the Adventure Game and singing and dancing /

Anna (*to* **Dwight**) I can see all the records over there, Dwight. D'you want to show me your favourite one? (**Anna** *stands and holds out her hand.*) C'mon.

Young Shirley *blocks her.*

Young Shirley He doesn't like strangers touching him.

Beat.

Anna Well, that must be hard at school, Dwight. Kids don't always know when to stop.

Young Shirley I tell them to stop, especially when they call him names.

Anna (*to* **Dwight**) What names do they call you?

Young Shirley   They say nasty things.

Anna   Shirley, can Dwight tell me himself please?

Beat.

Anna   What names do they call you, Dwight?

Beat.

Dwight   Freak. Schizo. Spaz. Weirdo.

Young Shirley   You're not a weirdo.

Dwight   You call me a weirdo /

Young Shirley   Not in that way. I fight everyone that picks on you.

Anna   You really shouldn't be fighting in school, Shirley?

Young Shirley   I'm his big sister. I have to look out for him when people say he can't do anything. Mum always says he can do everything.

Anna   Well no one can do everything, even mums and dads. They need special help too, some more than others. Your mum works at the hospital, right?

Young Shirley   Yeah.

Anna   That's a very busy, busy job. And what does your dad do?

Young Shirley   He used to work at the factory.

She makes a note.

Anna   Losing your job can be really upsetting. A lot of mums and dads are finding things really stressful lately. It can make them not nice to be around. (*Beat.*) Does your mum ever get sad or angry?

Dwight   Mum's a happy person.

Anna (*to* **Dwight**)   I heard she got angry with you at Woolworths. /

Young Shirley   How'd you know about that?

Anna *ignores* **Young Shirley** *and leans into* **Dwight**.

Anna   Mr Campbell said she got very upset with you. /

Young Shirley   That's not what I told him.

Anna   You said she pinched him.

Young Shirley   Not in a bad way.

Anna   Hurting someone in anyway is bad. /

Dwight (*shouts*)   My mum's not a bad person! /

Dwight *starts stimming out of worry and anxiousness.*

Anna   I'm not trying to make you upset. /

Dwight (*shouts*)   I don't want to talk to you anymore!

Young Shirley   Me too.

Josephine *rushes in, followed by* **Leroy**. *She embraces* **Dwight**.

Josephine   What did you say to him?

Anna   I didn't mean to upset him.

Leroy   It's time for you to go.

Anna   Mr and Mrs Williams, I have some concerns.

Josephine   Convcerns about what?

Anna   I spoke to the school and they are worried about the well-being of your children too, especially with Dwight's difficult needs.

Josephine   Dwight is not difficult. /

Anna   Children with mental retardation /

Josephine   Dwight is not retarded /

Anna   His delays are putting a strain on Shirley's behaviour at school. You work long hours and there's unsupervised alone time. (*Refers to* **Leroy**.) And I hear you're recently out of work.

Leroy   I take care of my family. (*Beat.*) Put that in your report and go. (*Beat.*) Now.

Beat. **Anna** *gathers her belongings.* **Josephine** *shows her out.* **Young Shirley** *keeps her distance from her father. Beat.* **Josephine** *rushes in and heads straight for* **Young Shirley**.

Josephine   What have you been saying at school? /

Young Shirley *backs away.*

Young Shirley   Nothing. I promise. /

Leroy   The social doesn't come around for nothing, Shirley.

Josephine   I tell you all the time to watch your mouth, but you get too excited making up stories.

Young Shirley   You're the one that pinched Dwight in the shop. /

Leroy (*to* **Josephine**)   You pinched Dwight?

Josephine (*to* **Young Shirley**)   When?

Young Shirley   That time when we went to buy him new school trousers.

Leroy (*to* **Josephine**)   Somebody saw you?

Josephine (*to* **Leroy**)   No one that knows who we are or where we live.

Leroy (*to* **Josephine**)   So how did they end up coming here?

Beat.

Young Shirley   I told Mr Campbell.

They turn to **Young Shirley**. *Beat.* **Josephine** *suddenly lunges at* **Young Shirley**.

Josephine   What have I told you about chatting our family business?

Young Shirley   He was laughing when I told him the story. /

Leroy   Yuh cyaa truss white people even eff dem laughing wid yuh!

Josephine *softly approaches* **Dwight**.

Josephine (*to* **Dwight**)   Dwight, tell me, has Mr Campbell asked you any questions? Has he said anything bad to you?

Beat.

Dwight   Dwight is a problem. Dwight doesn't belong here. He belongs in a special school.

Josephine *looks at* **Leroy**.

Josephine   Leroy, Mrs Harris promised Dwight would be welcomed at Bexley. She promised his needs would be championed for.

Leroy   She tried until they pushed her out for being vocal. There's no way the other black teachers would risk their jobs too.

Josephine   The government is talking about passing a law to get all disabled children into mainstream schools by the end of the year.

Leroy   Since when has the law treated us fairly?

Josephine   Dwight wasn't learning anything in those special schools, Leroy.

Leroy   You let Mrs Harris convince you that change was here.

Josephine   I don't need I told you so's. I'm going to speak to the head teacher.

Leroy   Josie, we need your job. And if you go in there screaming, the school will use it as an excuse to call the police and push things even further with the social.

Josephine   I don't want Dwight going in until it's sorted.

Leroy   They'll mark him down as a truant.

Josephine   Then you'd better go in today or you'll be home schooling him from now on. (*She takes the car keys from her handbag. To* **Leroy**.) Dwight will go with you today /

Leroy   Josie, I have a list of jobs from Curtis lined up.

Josephine   I don't want to hear it, Leroy. As long as he has his cassettes, he'll be fine. I'll take the bus to work. Pick me up after. And call the ward on my on my lunch. I want to know what Mr Campbell has to say for himself.

Young Shirley   Can I stay home with Dad too?

Josephine   No! You're going to school and you're going to keep your head down and mouth shut. (*To* **Leroy**.) Where will you be this afternoon?

Leroy   Probably Curtis's.

Josephine (*to* **Young Shirley**)   You go straight there. /

Young Shirley   But Rachel is not my friend anymore /

Josephine   Mi neva aks, Shirley! Go get your things.

Shirley *and* **Josephine** *exit.* **Dwight** *grabs his belongings and follows them.* **Leroy** *pulls him back.*

Leroy   You heard your mother. You're staying home. (**Dwight** *reacts and drops his bag and jacket.*) Okay. (**Leroy** *quickly lets go. The change in routine unsettles* **Dwight**.) She didn't give me much choice either. (**Dwight** *is about to start stimming.*) C'mon, don't do that. Here, pick your music. (**Leroy** *goes to the record player and turns it on. He doesn't realise the volume is high.* **Dwight** *screams and covers his ears.*) Dammit. (**Leroy** *quickly turns it off.* **Dwight** *starts stimming out of irritation. He needs reassuring.* **Leroy** *is awkward.* (*Beat.*) I always tell you to leave the volume button alone. Now, you've upset yourself. (*Beat.*) Is this what you've been doing for these teachers? (*Beat.*) I'm not your mother. I'm not going to hold you like some baby. (**Leroy** *is calculating how to approach and comfort* **Dwight**.) You're not the only one you know. You've got to learn how to keep it inside. (*Beat.*) We

have to . . . (*Beat. He makes contact with* **Dwight**.) The world
doesn't like us acting out. They'll put you down any chance
they get. You can't be doing all this screaming. You're a black
man, Dwight.

Beat. **Dwight** *looks at* **Leroy** *for a moment.*

Dwight   I'm a boy, Dad.

Leroy *is taken aback by* **Dwight**'*s correction. They hold their gaze
for a moment before* **Leroy** *pulls away.*

Leroy   Pack what you need.

Leroy *exits.* **Dwight** *picks up his backpack and takes out a vintage
car radio. He tunes the knobs. Static is heard.* **Dwight** *presses
various buttons. Snippets from each radio station is heard. It's a
soundscape of various programmes.*

Voices on the Radio (*woman's voice*)   Now on Radio 4, it's
time for Money Box with Louse Botting. (**Dwight** *changes the
station. Classical music plays. He doesn't like it. He changes the
station. He hears the BBC Radio One Newsbeat theme. He changes
the station. A man's voice is heard.*) Okay, assuming you are still
here listening to Our Tune our next story comes from a
married woman who recently discovered her husband's
affair. (**Dwight** *changes the station. It lands on Shakin' Stevens'
'You Drive Me Crazy'. A snippet of the song is played.* **Dwight** *sings
along.*)

Dwight *presses a button. The song gets cut off.*

Dwight (*mimicking* **Leroy**)   Dwight, you're driving me crazy.
Leave the goddam radio alone. When we stop here, you stay
in the car whilst I go fix this woman's refrigerator. This is
Roundhay. You can't be actin foolish inna dem yah white
people's driveway. Play your cassette.

Dwight *presses a button. A snippet of Linton Kwezi Johnson's*
Inglan is a Bitch *is played.*

Voices on the Radio   Inglan is a bitch /

Dwight *presses a button. The song gets cut off.*

Dwight (*mimicking* **Leroy**)   Turn it down! (*Beat.*) And wen yuh thief mi cassette?! Yuh betta nuh let yuh mother ketch yuh wid dat. Eat your lunch. I'll be right back.

Dwight *quickly presses the buttons on the radio. A piano is heard.*

Voices on the Radio (*man's voice*)   This afternoon's Pianist in Profile is Emil Gilels. A teenage virtuoso born to a Jewish family in Odessa, Ukraine. (**Dwight** *changes the station.*) Now, the evening news and sport on BBC Radio 2.

Dwight *changes in the station. Michael Jackson's 'One Day in Your Life' plays.* **Dwight** *leaves it. He returns the radio into his bag. He puts on his jacket on.*

Dwight   It's dinner time. Let's go, Dad. It's dinner time. Let's go, Shirley. I want to go home. I want to go home. No, I don't want rice. The soup is touching the rice. It's Monday. Mum makes mash potatoes and sausages for dinner. I want to go home. Let's go home, Shirley. Shirley, let's go home. I want to go home. (*The lights dim. Streetlights appear. Beat.*) I know the way home. (*He puts on his backpack.*) Right, right on Hamilton Place. Left on Louis Street. Right on Chapeltown Road. Walk past GB Stores, past Roscoe Methodist Church. Past Abdul's All Night Curry Center. Past the laundrette. Past Rosenhead Butcher. Turn left on Mexborough Grove.

A **Police Officer** *enters. He blocks* **Dwight**'s *path.*

Dwight   Turn left on Mexborough Grove.

Dwight *steps aside. The* **Police Officer** *mirrors him.* **Dwight** *is agitated. He's about to start stimming.*

Police Officer   Where'd you come from?

Dwight   Turn left on Mexborough Grove.

Dwight's *stimming is noticeable to the* **Police Officer**.

Police Officer   What's wrong with you? Got something in your bag that you shouldn't have? (**Dwight** *turns back to walk* *the opposite the direction The* **Police Officer** *yanks at* **Dwight's** *bag. His stimming intensifies.* **Dwight** *turns to leave.*) Oi, did I say you could go? (**Dwight** *and the* **Police Officer** *struggle over the backpack.* **Dwight** *slides out. The* **Police Officer** *stumbles.* **Dwight** *escapes.*) Come back here you little wog!

Dwight *exits. The* **Police Officer** *chases him.*

Scene Six

The Williams' House, *June 1981*

Lights up on the dining room. There's a table and chairs. A telephone sits in the corner. **Shirley** *enters and looks around her childhood home. She turns to see* **Young Shirley** *rushing in. She's still wearing her school uniform.*

Young Shirley   Dwight? D, are you here?

She exits to check upstairs. **Leroy** *enters. He's dressed in oil-stained overalls. The phone rings. He answers.*

Leroy   Hello? . . . Did he come back? . . . Shit . . . Pauline, Pauline stop, it's not your fault. He was fussing all day. I pushed my luck. I should have just brought him straight back home after my second job, but the Roundhay job was supposed to be a quick one. (*Beat.*) Is Curtis back? Okay, when he comes, tell him to go check Potternewton Park. I'll go towards town. Maybe he went to the infirmary for Josie . . . No, no, no you stay there in case he doubles back. Okay, bye. (*He hangs up. Yells up.*) Shirley?!

Young Shirley *returns.*

Leroy   Is he here?

Young Shirley   No.

Leroy   Shit.

Young Shirley   I told you that he doesn't have a key. He goes with Mum everywhere.

Leroy I told you to keep an eye on him.

Young Shirley I left him in kitchen with Aunty Pauline. /

Leroy You know he doesn't settle in people's homes.

Young Shirley Why am I in trouble? Dwight's the one that's run off. I was playing upstairs with Rachel.

Leroy You said you and Rachel weren't friends anymore.

Young Shirley She gave me sherbet lemons and a new My Guy magazine.

Leroy You should have taken him upstairs with you. /

Young Shirley You said he shouldn't be playing in girl's bedrooms. You could have taken him to the cellar with Uncle Curtis.

Leroy *leans in to smack her. She quickly moves out of the way. Beat.*

Leroy Don't talk back tuh mi like dat. Mi nuh one of yuh likkle friends.

Beat.

Young Shirley Should we call Mum? /

Leroy No. (*Beat.*) Go ask the neighbours if they've seen him.

Young Shirley *exits. The phone rings.*

Leroy Curtis? (*Beat.*) Oh Samson . . . no you don't have to come out. It's late . . . Well, Pauline shouldn't have woken you and Leanne . . . No, I will call my wife if I have to. I don't need you panicking her for nothing . . . Of course I know it's not nothing, I read the papers too . . . Samson, you're not the only one troubled by the NF. Plenty businesses and shops have had brick through. Just stay home and do your little prayers. I will find my son. (**Leroy** *slams the receiver down and kisses his teeth.* **Young Shirley** *returns.*)

Young Shirley   No one answered the door.

Leroy   He couldn't have walked far. Stay by the phone. If your mother calls tell her he's sleeping and I'm in the toilet.

Leroy *exits.* **Young Shirley** *sits on a chair.* **Shirley** *sits beside her. Beat. The phone rings.* **Young Shirley** *answers.* **Shirley** *watches her.*

Young Shirley (*tentatively*)   Hello? (*She exhales.*) You bloody scared me, Calvin. I thought you were my mum . . . I don't know. He just took off . . . I can't come out . . . My dad's not here . . . Because Calvin, I don't want to! I just want to be by myself.

She hangs up and exits. Lights down on the telephone. The chairs remain.

Shirley *is alone on stage. She is back in the present day in the Church of God of Prophecy.* **Calvin** *enters and sits beside her* **Shirley**. *She doesn't speak to him. They sit quietly for a moment.*

Calvin   Between you and your brother, I can't tell who's best at the silent treatment.

Shirley   I just want to be by myself, Calvin.

Calvin   Dwight is my family too. I'm not agency staff that you can clock me in and out of his life when it suits you. I promised your mum in the hospital I'd look out for him.

Shirley   Cos I do such a bad job? /

Calvin   Cos she knew you'd be missing her too. (*Beat.*) We had a plan. We were going to ask him to move in with us. What changed?

Beat.

Shirley   I'm nothing like Mum.

Calvin   He doesn't need you to be. He needs you to be his sister.

Shirley   I haven't always done a good job.

Calvin   C'mon, I take back what I said.

Shirley   Maybe you shouldn't. I weren't always nice to him when we were kids.

Calvin   Siblings fight /

Shirley   Stop saying that, Cal. I'm not a good person. I did something and I never told anyone.

Beat.

Calvin   What did you do?

Beat.

Shirley   D'you remember that time, when we were kids and Dwight disappeared?

Calvin   Yeah.

Shirley   That night, it was my fault.

Calvin   No. Leroy lost him. He'd been busy playing dominoes in Curtis' basement.

Shirley   And I was upstairs with Rachel. (*Beat.*) I came back down, Cal. (*Beat.*) I'd left my bag in the kitchen. Me and Rachel had made up. I wanted to show Rachel the lipstick I'd nicked from Mum. I heard Aunty Pauline in the basement. Dwight was by himself. I could tell he was tired and wanted to go home. I wasn't ready to go. He just kept pulling at me. Everything was always on his time. Dad was busy telling everyone that I brought the social to the house. No one asked for my side of the story. No one cared about how I was feeling. I was protecting him from Mr Campbell and I got in trouble for it.

Calvin   It wasn't your fault that racist teacher took what he wanted from your story.

Shirley   Aunty Pauline always felt bad that she forget to lock the door, but she didn't. (*Beat.*) It was me. I unlocked it. (*Beat.*) I just wanted him away from me. I didn't want to go

home. I told him that he ruins things . . . I told him that I
wanted him just to disappear. I left it open and I went back
upstairs. (*Pause.*) Say something.

Beat.

Calvin   Why didn't you tell me any of this?

Shirley   How do I tell you about the worst thing I've ever
done?

Calvin   You tell me like you're telling me now.

Shirley   I wanted to but /

Calvin   But what? You couldn't find a moment in the last
forty years? You're unbelievable you know. This whole thing.
Selling our house, moving into your mum's, the silent
treatment. This has nothing to do with what Dwight needs.
It's all about you. You and your bloody need to control
everything, even how we all feel about you.

Shirley   When do I ever control how you feel?

Calvin   You're dropping this information right now so that
I can't be mad at you at your mum's funeral. Do you realise
how messed up this is? You need to talk to your brother
before you upturn everything that I've bloody worked for.

Shirley   How do I even begin? Things got worse for us
when he went missing. I was always too afraid to ask him
what they did to him. I couldn't bear the thought of it.

Calvin   You're not the only one that's had to confront their
pain, Shirley. Your mother had to. Leroy had to. Dwight
certainly has faced his fair share of demons. Shit, I've got my
own too. You don't get to ignore yours.

Shirley   What pain do you have?

Beat.

Calvin   I have little cuts.

Shirley   What?

Calvin   Little cuts that you keep tearing open /

Shirley   Give me an example.

Calvin   The shop, the boys. You throw away the idea of them like as if they don't mean anything to me. I like spending time with them. I like being able to mentor them and watch them grow like as if they're /

Shirley   Your own children? (*Beat.*) You could have left me.

Calvin   I never wanted to leave you.

Shirley   I decided a long time ago that I didn't want to be a mother.

Calvin   I accepted that.

Shirley   Your family never did.

Calvin   You were my woman to choose.

Beat.

Shirley   Are you happy with how your life's turned out?

Beat.

Calvin   Are you asking me or yourself? (*Beat.*) Bury whatever guilt you've been carrying over Dwight all these years, Shirley, because I'm not sure how much longer I can keep mending my wounds for the sake of loving you.

Calvin *leaves.* **Shirley** *remains on stage.*

Act Two

Scene One

Meanwood Park Hospital, *June 1981*

Spotlight on **Dwight**. **Shirley** *remains on stage. He paces in a confined box. He's trapped. This is both a memory for* **Dwight** *and what* **Shirley** *feared of* **Dwight**'s *experiences. There is a cacophony of voices and clambering. Each sound startles him. He covers his ears.*

Dwight (*calls out*) Shirley? Shirley? SHIRLEY? I want to go home. Let me go home. Let me go home. Thirty-four Mexborough Mount, LS7 3DZ. Shirley, let's go home. (*Screams out.*) SHIRLEY! (*His stimming is frequent and intense. Lights up on the waiting room. There are four chairs and a small side table with magazines.* **Young Shirley** *is pacing.*) Dwight lives at home with Mummy, Daddy and Shirley. Dwight lives at home with Mummy, Daddy and Shirley.

Shirley *is overwhelmed. She exits as* **Anna** *enters. Lights down on* **Dwight**. **Young Shirley** *notices her. She stops pacing. They sit in silence.* **Young Shirley** *picks up a magazine. Beat.* **Anna** *picks up a magazine too. Beat.* **Anna** *tries to play peek-a-boo with her.*

Young Shirley I'm not a baby.

Anna She speaks.

Young Shirley I'm not talking to you.

Anna *puts her magazine down.*

Anna I wish you would.

Young Shirley Why? So that you can make up more lies about my family? We can't trust white people. You're all liars.

Anna I haven't lied to you about anything.

Young Shirley   You believed Mr Campbell's twisted lies about my mum. Now everything's all messed up and Dwight's locked up in here.

Anna *moves beside her.*

Anna   Shirley, I came into this job to help families, not mess things up.

Leroy *enters.* **Young Shirley** *moves away from* **Anna**.

Leroy (*to* **Young Shirley**)   Have they brought him out?

Young Shirley   No.

Anna   Mr Williams /

Leroy   I don't have time for you right now. I just came to get my son.

Anna   Is Mrs Williams /

Josephine *enters. She's still wearing her uniform.*

Josephine   Have they brought him out yet? /

Leroy   No. /

Josephine   Shirley, ring the bell.

Young Shirley   I pressed it already, but no one's come to the window yet.

Josephine   What kind of place doesn't have someone by reception?

Anna   It usually takes a while. It's a big hospital.

Josephine   Did you bring another referral to get him out?

Beat.

Anna   No.

Josephine   Then you can go.

Anna   Can we have a word? /

Josephine I'm dun chatting tuh yuh people. I just want my child and to go home.

Anna There's procedures /

Josephine Mi nuh gi a damn bout procedures!

Anna Dwight wouldn't stop kicking and screaming. He wouldn't answer any of the police's questions. /

Leroy Stop and search is not questioning.

Anna He assaulted an officer. /

Leroy He's a child. /

Josephine Dwight would never hurt anyone on purpose.

Anna They didn't know what was wrong with him. He wouldn't talk to them. Meanwood Park Hospital seemed the safest place for him.

Leroy They kidnapped him off the street.

Josephine They had no right to bring him here.

Anna The mental health act gives police /

Josephine I've told you already. Dwight is not sick in his head. (*To* **Young Shirley**.) Shirley, press that bell again. /

Anna Mrs Williams /

Josephine I want him discharged.

Anna It doesn't work like that. /

Josephine I work in a hospital. Patients get admitted and discharged.

Anna There's a minimum twenty-four-hour hold with psychiatric patients. Pending a review of his assessment, a decision will be made on his residence /

Josephine Residence?

Anna   In some cases, the hold can be extended for up to twenty-eight days /

Young Shirley   You can't keep my brother here. What about school?

Anna   There's a school here. (*To* **Josephine**.) Other children like Dwight thrive living here /

Josephine   Little girl. I'll say this one more time. Dwight has a home. And we were doing just fine before you barged into our lives.

Anna   Dwight wasn't taken from your home, Mrs Williams. He was wandering the streets alone late last night. (**Josephine** *and* **Leroy** *exchange looks. Beat.*) He wasn't in school yesterday. Shirley is not in today.

Beat.

Leroy   Shirley was too upset to go and we wanted to resolve any issues with the school before sending Dwight back.

Anna   Mr Campbell didn't mention a meeting.

Leroy *feels the weight of* **Josephine**'s *stare. Beat.*

Leroy   I had to juggle a few things with work and Dwight wouldn't settle. I didn't want him to see the school, especially when he wouldn't be staying. It would have confused him. The day just got away from me. I was going to speak to Mr Campbell today but, here we are.

Josephine (*to* **Anna**)   Go find out what's keeping them. (*Beat.*) Please.

Anna   I'll see what I can do.

Anna *exits. Silence.* **Leroy** *is waiting for a response from* **Josephine**. *She doesn't speak.*

Leroy   The music helped for a little while and then he started playing with the radio and shaking the car, wanting to get out. I'll have to take a look at the suspension later today. (**Josephine** *doesn't respond.*) I went to Curtis to talk about a new business venture. I want to work for myself fixing things. Curtis can find me clients. Josie, we can't survive if I'm just doing little piece jobs. Dwight was fine once Shirley come off school. The sound system was going in the basement. Everything was fine. (**Josephine** *doesn't respond.*) Me and Curtis looked everywhere for him. I told Samson not to call you /

Josephine That's my child, Leroy! Nothing matters more than him. You should have called me the second you realised that back door was open.

Leroy He could have just been in the back garden /

Josephine But he wasn't, Leroy! He's in a secure ward /

Leroy You turn your back too Josie. You go to the toilet. You go to the salon. You go to church. You go to Kirkgate. You can lose him anytime, anywhere too. /

Josephine But I haven't, not once, in all his life.

Leroy Mi cya neva win wid yuh! /

Josephine Nobody is winning! /

Leroy The police snatch him off the street with nobody in sight to say who he belongs to /

Josephine He belongs to you! (*Beat.*) It's your job to protect him. But you couldn't even keep that like the damn factory job.

Silence. **Anna** *returns.*

Anna Okay, so visiting hours are on Saturdays /

Josephine I didn't ask you to check the visiting hours. (*She pushes past* **Anna**.) I have to do everything myself /

Anna Security will remove you without seeing Dwight. (**Josephine** *stops.*) If you'd let me finish, I would have told you that they've agreed for me to take you onto the ward for a few minutes. You'll have to leave your personal belongings with your husband.

Josephine   Shirley, take my bag.

Young Shirley   I want to see Dwight too. /

Anna   Children are not allowed on the ward.

Young Shirley   Mum?

Josephine   What?

Beat.

Young Shirley   Tell Dwight. (*Beat.*) Tell him I miss him, and I want him to come home.

Anna *and* **Josephine** *exit. Beat.*

Young Shirley   Dad?

Leroy   What?

Beat.

Young Shirley   Is Dwight going to be okay?

Leroy   You heard your mother, she'll sort it.

Young Shirley   Daddy?

Leroy   What is it, Shirley?

Beat.

Young Shirley   I should have let him play with me and Rachel. I'm sorry.

Leroy   It's not your fault. (*Beat.*) C'mon. Let's go wait in the car.

They exit.

Scene Two

Ward 48, Meanwood Park Hospital, *June 1981*

Lights up on a metal frame bed with a thin mattress. **Dwight** *is underneath covered by grey worn-out hospital bedding. He's shut down and silent.* **Anna** *and* **Josephine** *enter.*

Josephine I thought you said he was in here.

Anna This is the ward number they gave me.

Josephine Patients are supposed to be admitted according to their needs. There's men twice his size banging their heads in the corridors.

Anna This must have been the only available bed last night.

Josephine *kneels down and looks under the bed. She tugs at the bedding.* **Dwight** *pulls it back.*

Josephine Dwight? (*To* **Anna**.) What's he doing under the bed? (*To* **Dwight**.) Dwight, please come out. (*She reaches under the bed to touch him. He pushes her hand away.*) D, it's me. It's Mummy. (*He doesn't move. To* **Anna**.) Help me with the bed. (**Dwight** *is revealed.* **Josephine** *slowly lifts the blanket and lies down beside him. Beat.*) Dwight, look at me. I'm here. I'm going to take you home. (*To* **Anna**.) He looks so tired.

Anna The tranquiliser must be wearing off.

Josephine They drugged my child?

Anna The nurse said he was hystetical.

Josephine He's never taken anything more than a paracetamol.

Dwight (*muttering to himself*) Two sleeps and then Shirley is coming home from camping. Twenty sleeps and then Dad is coming home from Jamaica. Three sleeps and then Calvin is home from football training.

Josephine You'll be back in your own bed very soon. I promise. (*To* **Anna**.) I don't what him sleeping here another night. I want him out today.

Anna *watches* **Josephine** *tend to* **Dwight** *for a moment. Beat.*

Anna We should go.

Josephine We've barely been here two minutes.

Anna   I don't want to push it. We need the hospital on our side.

Josephine   I shouldn't have to pander to them to see my child. They have him dashed on an ice-cold floor like as if he doesn't belong to anybody who cares about him.

Anna   I don't think they would have done it intentionally.

Josephine   Plenty things are done unintentionally. It doesn't make them right.

Beat.

Anna   I'm trying my best, Mrs Williams. You're my first family. You have to give me a chance to do my job.

Josephine   It's time to take off your training wheels and open your eyes, Anna /

Anna   My eyes are open /

Josephine   Saying procedures every two second is not the job. (*She points at* **Dwight**.) My son is the job.

Anna   I put everything aside to call around the police stations and hospitals. Believe it or not, I'm on your side. I'm Dwight's advocate /

Josephine   I am Dwight's advocate! He came out of my body, not yours /

Anna   I didn't mean to imply that /

Josephine   You white people /

Anna   Please, this isn't about race. I'm here to help Dwight.

Josephine   You don't offer help. (*Beat.*) You want control. Ever since I first asked the GP why Dwight felt the world differently, you people have always wanted me to say that something is medically wrong with him just so that you can have another black body to experiment a cure on. I refused then and I refuse now. (*Beat. She tends to* **Dwight** *by lifting him off the floor and onto the bed.*) I may not be a doctor, but my gut knows your assessments of Dwight have always been wrong. I just want him back home.

The Medical Officer at the infirmary saw him when he was six years old. But I wouldn't call what he did an assessment. He poked, prodded, and made loud noises in Dwight's ears for all of five minutes, then turned around and said in his medical opinion I must have caught a virus during pregnancy and deformed his brain. I told him I'd been perfectly healthy. I did nothing different carrying Dwight, than what I did for Shirley. Then he said it must have be my food, my house or my accent because nurture affects development too. He'd decided that he didn't want to help people like us long before we set foot in his office. (*Beat.*) Dwight is not incompetent or deformed. When he shuts down like this, I can always pull him back to me by the grace of God. (*Beat.* **Josephine** *is upset.*) They won't do that for him in here.

Beat.

Anna   Did the Medical Officer send you a written assessment after the appointment?

Josephine   Why?

Anna   Doctors listen to doctors.

Josephine   They should be listening to me.

Anna   Meanwood has no records of Dwight. But, if you have a letter at home we could answer a few questions about him and start to move things along. (*Beat.*) We can work together.

Beat.

Josephine   What if I don't find it?

Anna   It's worth a try. (**Josephine** *turns to* **Dwight**. *Beat.*) Josephine, sorry Mrs Williams, we really do have to leave.

Beat.

Josephine (*to* **Dwight**)   Look at my fingers, D, (*She counts.*) Wednesday, Thursday, Friday and Saturday. Four days and I'll come back. Okay? (*Beat.*) Shirley wants you back too.

Josephine *kisses him. She gets up and exits. Beat.* **Anna** *looks at* **Dwight**.

Anna   I'll come back, I promise.

Anna *exits.*

Dwight   I'll come back. (*Beat.*) 'I'll Come Back to You'. 1980. Larry and Laura Santos.

Dwight *sings the song and repeats a line from the chorus.*

> Come back
> Come back
> Come back, Dwight.

He pulls the covers down again. Lights fade on **Dwight**.

Scene Three

Bexley Middle School, *July 1981*

Young Shirley *enters and crosses the stage.* **Mr Campbell** *follows her ringing the school bell.*

Mr Campbell   Your classroom is the opposite direction. (*She ignores him and keeps on walking.*) Shirley? (*Beat.*) That's detention.

She stops and turns around.

Young Shirley   For what?

Mr Campbell   That attitude first. (*She kisses her teeth.*) D'you want another one?

Young Shirley   For kissing my teeth?

Mr Campbell   Your behaviour lately is very disappointing.

Young Shirley   God, why are you always stalking me?

Mr Campbell   This is my school. I keep track of everyone.

Young Shirley   Those boys are pissing about and you said nothing.

Mr Campbell   I don't have reports piled high on my desk about them starting fights in lessons.

Young Shirley   I was defending myself.

Mr Campbell   The smart thing is to always walk away from bullies.

Young Shirley   I'm trying to but you keep following me.

Mr Campbell   Watch yourself. You're heading for a suspension at this rate.

Young Shirley   Why am I the one getting suspended? People are saying nasty things about Dwight and that I'll be taken next. This is all your fault.

Mr Campbell   Shirley, you're young. You can't see it now but I was helping you. /

Young Shirley   I wish people would stop saying that! I'm never, ever asking for help. I hate this school now. You've made it worse.

Mr Campbell   Her Majesty's Inspectorate disagrees. Our rating has gone up. (*Beat.*) Striving to learn, improve and grow together. That is our new ethos. Get on board if you want to fit in.

Young Shirley   Or what? You'll kick me out too?

Mr Campbell   That's up to you. But I bet you don't want to be out truanting and run into the police too. (*Beat.*) You have a real opportunity here, Shirley. Don't squander it.

Beat. **Shirley** *steps closer to him.*

Young Shirley   One day, I am going to come back to this school, and I'm not going to be a teacher, or a stupid deputy head. I'm going to be the head teacher and you're going to be fired.

Beat.

Mr Campbell   I'm giving you the summer holidays to fix your attitude.

Mr Campbell *exits. Beat.* **Young Shirley** *exits.*

Scene Four

The Williams' House, *July 1981*

Afternoon. Lights up on the dining table, sofa, display cabinet and telephone. **Leroy** *rushes in carrying a box of flyers with a megaphone inside. He plays 'The Harder They Come' by Jimmy Cliff on the record player.* **Young Shirley** *enters. They dance together. The phone rings.* **Leroy** *answers it.*

Leroy (*on the phone*)   Hello? . . . yeah, yeah I'm ready. I'll meet you by Hayfield's . . . How many did you recruit? . . . Good, good, twenty is good . . . Yeah, I got the flyers printed. (*He takes out a flyer and looks at it.*) They look real good.

Josephine *enters wearing a dressing gown. She's carrying a box filled with papers. She places them on the table and cuts off the music.*

Leroy   I'll keep some boys with me in Chapeltown. You take the rest canvassing in Harehills and Hyde Park . . . No, I didn't ask him . . . You can pass by the barber shop if you want, but I already know what Samson is going to say. Him nuh like getting fi him hands dirty unless it's dandruff. (*He laughs.*) That's right, trouble needs troubling to put the streets right.

Josephine *kisses her teeth and exits.* **Young Shirley** *enters carrying a second box. She's out of her school uniform. Her t-shirt reads 'FREEDOM' in coloured pens. She places the box on the table.* **Young Shirley** *picks up the megaphone and tests it out.*

Young Shirley   No justice! No peace! No racist police!

Leroy *smiles proudly.*

Leroy (*on the phone*)   Yes, that's Shirley. We'll have the whole community chanting it.

Young Shirley (*leans into the phone*)   Uncle Curtis, is Rachel wearing her t-shirt too?

Beat.

Leroy (*to* **Young Shirley**)   She is.

Josephine *enters with a third box of papers.*

Leroy (*on the phone*)   Listen, remember that white boy Max Farrar that takes pictures and writes for the *Chapeltown News*? . . . He asked to meet us at Hayfield's. He wants to do a little story on the police patrol in the community . . . enough is enough. Right, soon. (*He hangs up. To* **Shirley**.) Let's go. /

Josephine (*to* **Young Shirley**)   I told you to get started on these boxes.

Young Shirley   But I'm going out with Dad.

Josephine   I didn't ask.

Young Shirley   But /

Josephine   But, but what?

Leroy   Josie, you looked through those boxes already.

Josephine *ignores him.*

Young Shirley   Dad?

Leroy   Josephine, give the child a break. /

Young Shirley   The letter is not in here. /

Josephine (*snaps*)   It's in here! /

Young Shirley   It's not. /

Josephine *repeatedly slams the boxes on the table.*

Josephine   Shirley, shut up! Just shut up! (*Beat. She composes herself.*) I'm certain I received one. It says, NHS, August 1976 on the top righthand corner and his signature is crooked, looked like when Dwight first started writing.

Josephine *ignores him. She pours out the papers from the boxes.*

Leroy   Did you call work to tell them you weren't going in again?

Josephine (*to* **Young Shirley**)   Why are you just standing there? Start on these.

Leroy   Josie, it's the weekend. Let Shirley go see her friends.

Josephine   Don't you think Dwight would like play with his friends too? /

Young Shirley (*to herself*)   What friends?

Josephine *hears.*

Josephine   God hears and sees everything, Shirley. Sort out those papers now.

Young Shirley *puts the megaphone back into* **Leroy**'s *box.* **Leroy** *steps closer to* **Josephine**.

Leroy   You need to get out of the house. Go see Pauline and Leanne for the afternoon. They have been asking after you.

Josephine   They could just as easily come here.

Leroy   They don't know how. You've locked yourself in here like a fortress and hang up on them when they call.

Josephine   The line can't be busy with nuisance calls.

Leroy   It's been two weeks. Anna is not going to call. We must act and reclaim our streets. We've got plenty black men out there. We need to see our black women too.

Josephine *goes to his box and picks up a flyer. She scans it.*

Josephine   I don't see Dwight's face on this. I don't read his name anywhere on these flyers. I haven't heard you talking about putting him in the *Chapeltown News* or calling out Meanwood Hospital.

Leroy   I'm organising the community today /

She throws the flyers at him.

Josephine   Dwight is the community!

Beat. He picks up the flyers.

Leroy   I know that. /

Josephine   Ha! /

Leroy   You don't believe me? /

Josephine   What happened last year with the Saturday school?

Leroy   What do you mean?

Josephine   Leanne came to you and said the Saturday School wasn't right for him and what did you do?

Leroy   She had ten other children to teach and he wouldn't sit down.

Josephine   You weren't even the one that put him in there. I did. But Leanne came to you because she knew you'd agree with her, instead of making sure Dwight learnt about Kush and Mary Seacole just like you're always pushing for Shirley to /

Leroy   Haven't I tried to teach him here?

Josephine   You yell. You're impatient. You don't listen to him. /

Leroy   I'm not you, Josie. I'm not going to make him soft. /

Josephine   There's nothing soft about being him. You don't recall the doctor, the nursery, the primary schools, the shopkeepers and the neighbours that complained about his screaming? You've never made flyers protesting all those people. You have never come to my defence when your sister asks why I don't discipline him. You never said anything when your mother visited and took him to the church to raise the demons out of him.

Leroy   I'm going to start picking small fights with every person that looks at Dwight the wrong way /

Josephine   It's not small, Leroy! /

Leroy   Compared to the police brutalising us? /

Josephine   They brutalised him too. (*Beat.*) They took him too. You don't see him. (*Beat.*) Sometimes, I watch how gentle Samson cuts Dwight's hair and it just makes me sad to think how Dwight has never known a father like that.

Pause. **Leroy** *nods silently and picks up his box.*

Leroy   Shirley, lets go. /

Josephine   Shirley, sit down.

Leroy *grabs* **Young Shirley**'*s arm.*

Leroy   I said come.

Josephine *pulls* **Young Shirley** *back and stands in front of her like a shield.*

Josephine (*to* **Leroy**)   I said no.

Young Shirley   I want to go with Dad.

Leroy   Josie, don't be stupid. You're upsetting the child.

Josephine   Just take your things and go.

Leroy *reaches for* **Young Shirley** *again.* **Josephine** *pushes him back. He drops the box.*

Leroy   Don't put your hands on me, Josie. /

Josephine *grabs a handful of flyers and throws them at* **Leroy**. *He remains composed.*

Josephine   Take your stupid flyers and go! /

Leroy   You're going to make me lose my temper.

She steps closer to him.

Josephine   You don't care about your family. (*She pushes him.*) Go! (*She pushes him again.*) Go on! (*She drives him out.*) Get ouuut!

Leroy *moves her back.* **Josephine** *pushes back harder. An alarm rings. A red light showers the stage.* **Leroy** *restrains her in a bid to calm the situation.* **Josephine** *starts hitting and punching* **Leroy**. *More papers and flyers rain down. Spotlight on* **Dwight**. *The alarms distress him. There's a cacophony of screams and clambering.*

Leroy   Have you lost your mind? /

Dwight   Make it stop! /

Young Shirley   Mum, stop! /

Dwight   It's too loud. /

Young Shirley   Dad, let her go.

Dwight's *stimming is intense.* **Leroy** *and* **Josephine** *struggle with each other.* **Anna** *enters and approaches* **Dwight**.

Anna (*to* **Dwight**)   What do you want me to do? Tell me, Dwight. What does your mum do?

Josephine *bites* **Dwight**. **Leroy** *pushes her to the group. He flips over the sofa. He picks up the box and megaphone. He exists.*

Young Shirley *approaches* **Josephine**. **Josephine** *smacks her. She's shocked by her own action. She gets up and leaves* **Young Shirley** *on the floor holding her cheque.* **Dwight** *recalls scripture recited to him by* **Josephine**.

Dwight (*mimics* **Josephine**)   Cast all your anxiety on him, Dwight, because he cares for you. Hold on to God.

Anna   What does that mean?

A **Police Officer** *enters and confronts* **Leroy**. *There's a standoff between them.* **Josephine** *wrestles* **Young Shirley** *to the ground.* **Dwight** *begins singing Mahalia Jackson 'His Eye is on the Sparrow'.* **Leroy** *reaches for the megaphone inside the box. The* **Police Officer** *draws his baton.* **Leroy** *aims the megaphone like a gun and gestures repeatedly as if he's firing.* **Leroy** *is arrested. The alarm stops.* **Dwight**'s *voice is heard singing.* **Anna** *listens to him for a moment.* **Young Shirley** *starts clearing up the living room. She beats the sofa cushions in anger.*

Dwight *continues to sing.*

Lights down on **Dwight**. **Anna** *turns to watch* **Young Shirley**.

Scene Five

The Williams' House, *July 1981*

Young Shirley *starts picking up the papers. She shoves them all into the boxes.* **Young Shirley** *notices* **Anna**. **Anna** *is surprised by the mess.*

Anna   I knocked.

Young Shirley *looks at her and continues cleaning.*

Young Shirley   What do you want?

Beat.

Anna   What happened in here?

Young Shirley   Mum's been looking for that letter you said could save Dwight.

Anna   Didn't the infirmary have a copy?

Young Shirley   We went down there to speak to the Medical Officer, but he didn't remember ever seeing Dwight or speaking to Mum. She called him a liar and they got into a fight. She'd already missed so much work, so they put her on suspension.

Anna   I'm sorry to hear that.

Beat.

Young Shirley   We've been calling you. Your office always says that you're out.

Anna   They've not been good at giving me messages lately.

Young Shirley   Why haven't you been calling us?

Beat.

Anna   I've had other families to help. /

Young Shirley   So, you just forgot about us?

Anna   I didn't forget. It's complicated, Shirley.

Young Shirley   Grown-ups say that when they don't want to tell you the truth.

Beat.

Anna   I made some people angry.

Young Shirley   How?

Anna   When I helped you all find Dwight, my manager thought that I got too involved. The police had done their job right. She said I needed to focus on my job and gave me another family in different neighbourhood to help.

Young Shirley   Just tell her that you don't want another family. /

Anna   It doesn't work like that. I'm new at my job. /

Young Shirley   I knew you were a liar. You were never going to help Dwight.

Anna   I tried.

Young Shirley   No, you didn't. You ran away.

Anna   It's not easy you know. I'm checking families' welfare, but no one seems to care about fixing their problems. The system's broken. No one will listen to me and I don't know what else I can do. I wanted to see your mum sooner but every time I drove by I'd end up just sitting outside in my car scared to come in.

Young Shirley   Mum says we have to do things scared sometimes because it makes us brave.

Anna   Well, I wasn't brave enough to see your mum with anything to show and plus your dad scares me.

Young Shirley   My dad's not scary. (*Beat.*) He just shouts a little.

Beat.

Anna   Are they in?

Beat.

Young Shirley   Mum's sleeping and the police arrested Dad.

Anna   What? Why?

Young Shirley   He was handing out flyers.

Anna   That's not a crime.

Young Shirley   It is around here.

Anna   Did your mum say when he's coming out?

Young Shirley   She hasn't been to see him.

Anna   Why?

Young Shirley   She doesn't want to. She even chased Uncle Curtis and Aunt Marcia away when they came here with a journalist who said he was wrongfully arrested. He had pictures to prove Dad didn't do anything. Mum wouldn't hear it. (*Beat.*) She won't even let me go out to play with Calvin and Rachel. She's mad at Aunty Pauline for leaving the door unlocked. Aunty Leanne thinks Mum's being unfair. School's about to close and I'll be alone all summer.

We all go to carnival together. Dwight really likes the music and the colours on the costumes. He's missing everything. (*Beat.*) I couldn't get Mum out of bed to go see him on the last visit. (*Beat.*) He was waiting, and no one showed up for him.

Anna   I showed up.

Young Shirley   You saw him?

Anna   Yeah.

Young Shirley   How is he?

Beat.

Anna   There was an incident with another patient /

Young Shirley   Someone hurt him? /

Anna   No. A fire alarm was pulled. The noise really scared him.

Young Shirley   We sing when he's upset.

Anna   He sang for me. He sang this song about a bird and being free.

Young Shirley   When I'm sad, Dwight can always make me happy. He finds the oddest things funny and cos he's laughing we all start laughing. (*Beat.*) No one's laughing here anymore.

Beat.

Anna   C'mon.

Young Shirley   Where are going?

Anna *starts picking up the papers.*

Anna   Your mum keeps a clean house. (**Young Shirley** *joins her.*) We're going to tidy it up and hopefully it'll make her happy. Then I'm going back to the office to make some calls to Meanwood Hospital.

Young Shirley   What if you get in trouble again?

Beat.

Anna   Do you know the name of the journalist that came over?

Young Shirley   Yeah. He's my dad's friend.

Anna   Maybe he can do a story on Dwight and I can talk about everyone who wouldn't help him.

Young Shirley   I want to be in it too.

Anna   We should probably ask your mum first.

Young Shirley   Okay.

Anna *exits. Lights fade on the house.* **Young Shirley** *remains on stage.*

Scene Six

Visitor Center, Armley Prison, *August 1981*

Two weeks later. **Josephine** *enters. She's well dressed and composed. She puts a coat onto* **Young Shirley**. *She straightens her up. The* **Prison Officer** *enters and places two chairs facing each other. The prison makes* **Young Shirley** *feel uncomfortable. She takes* **Josephine**'s *hand.* **Josephine** *squeezes her hand reassuringly.* **Leroy** *enters. He's wearing grey sweats.* **Josephine**, **Young Shirley** *and* **Leroy** *exchange looks.* **Leroy** *sits. Beat.* **Young Shirley** *and* **Josephine** *approach him.* **Josephine** *sits.* **Young Shirley** *stands closely behind her. Silence.*

Leroy   It's weird seeing me here isn't it, baby girl? (**Young Shirley** *nods. Beat.*) You don't have to be scared. It's still me, just different clothes. Okay? (**Leroy** *looks at* **Josephine**) You well?

Josephine   As can be.

Beat.

Leroy (*to* **Young Shirley**)   Carnival's soon. Have you got your costume sorted? Which troupe are you with?

Young Shirley   Mara Ya Pili Community Dance.

Josephine   Rachel and Calvin joined so she wanted to be with them.

Leroy   Curtis came to see me. He said you'd mended things with Leanne and Pauline.

Josephine   Well, it wasn't right for the children's friendships to suffer.

Leroy   That's good. That's good. The elders need to be an example for the children. (**Josephine** *scoffs and shakes her head. Beat.*) Shirley, can you go sit down by them chairs. I need to talk to your mother. (**Shirley** *sits near the* **Prison Officer**. *To* **Josephine**.) I wasn't sure if you were going to come see me.

Josephine   Well, Pauline said she would put a curse on me if I didn't.

Beat.

Leroy   I didn't go out there to make trouble, Josie. I'd be out of this place if the CPS wasn't trying to make an example out of me. They gave me two months for assault with intent to resist arrest. I never hit that police officer with the megaphone. He cried wolf just in time for his friends to show up. You know I wouldn't just hurt a man if it wasn't in self-defence. (**Leroy** *leans in to* **Josie** *again.*)

Leroy   You believe me, right?

Prison Officer   Sit back.

Leroy (*to the* **Prison Officer**)   C'mon man, I'm trying to talk to my woman. (*The* **Prison Officer** *stands.*) Alright, alright.

Beat. The **Prison Officer** *sits.* **Josephine** *watches him.* **Leroy** *sighs.*

Leroy   You see that? You see how he threatens me in front of you and Shirley? This is why Chapeltown burnt down. If I had been on the streets when the riots began, I would have /

Josephine   You would have done what?

Beat.

Leroy   I wouldn't have blamed them for causing damage. From Brixton to Toxteth to Handsworth to Moss Side we're angry. (**Josephine** *doesn't respond. She just watches him.*)

Leroy   I hate it when you go quiet. Say what's on your mind.

Beat.

Josephine   Aren't you tired?

Leroy   Of course, I'm tired. We've been dealing with the same hate from the police since me, you, Leanne, Samson, Curtis and Pauline came to this country. There's no progress! Just more strife that now our children gotta deal with. It's part of who they are.

Josephine   We can give them joy too.

Leroy   What joy can we give them when they can't even walk down their own streets? We need to remove the police or else our children will be murdered like David Oluwale was. Happily walking along the road one minute and then a bloated corpse in the River Aire the next. Is that what you want?

Josephine   People always tell that part of his life.

Leroy   It's a very important part.

Josephine   They also put him in Menston Asylum for eight years. They drugged him and gave him electroconvulsive therapy. (*Beat.*) He was a tailor with dreams and then he became a shell of himself until the day he was killed. (*Beat.*) Meanwood Park Hospital has already had Dwight for a month and a half. (*Beat.*) We've got to talk about that too,

Leroy. (*Beat.*) I'm tired of fighting you before we can go outside to fight against everybody else. You make being happy so difficult.

Beat.

Leroy   Well, sorry I'm not like Samson. Maybe you should be pick him in your next life.

Josephine   I never said I wanted him.

Leroy   You always find ways to compare me to him.

Josephine   I'll be trying to encourage you.

Leroy   By telling me to be like another husband, another father? (*Beat.*) What if I said that I wish you were more like Pauline? /

Josephine   Pushover Pauline? Please. /

Leroy   At least she speaks life into Curtis. /

Josephine   Tuh follow stupidness /

Leroy   They are a team. We're just /

Josephine   Just what?

Beat.

Leroy   Two people just surviving life together.

Beat.

Josephine   Right.

Leroy   Tell me I'm lying. (*Beat.*) Tell me where our love is. Tell me where our happiness is /

Josephine   In our children.

Leroy   We were man and woman before mother and father.

Josephine   Life changed when they were born.

Leroy   We lost ourselves long before we had them. They just came along and filled up the holes.

Josephine   Is that how you see your life? Filled with holes?

Leroy   I don't know /

Josephine   That's not good enough, Leroy! You asked me to come see you, so you'd better say something more than this.

Prison Officer   Keep your voices down.

Beat. They both sigh deeply.

Leroy   We're buried.

Josephine   In what?

Leroy   In life. (*Beat.*) In what we thought coming to England was going to be.

Josephine   You keep saying we. /

Leroy   Fine, me. It's all me. I feel buried. (*Pause.*) I've been thinking about my father a lot lately. (*Beat.*) About how I was supposed to give a meaning to his hardships by coming to England to excel. (*Beat.*) The queen's country is rough you know. (*Beat.*) It's sanded down the man my father wanted me to become and underneath, is this exposed, raw flesh of a man who is –

Beat.

Josephine   Who is what?

Beat.

Leroy   Not sure of who he is.

Josephine   I warned you about copying your father.

Leroy   Who else is supposed to teach me how to act, how to be, if not the generation before?

Josephine   Look where we are. Do you really think they did a good job with us?

Leroy   You've come out on top.

Josephine   I find plenty things hard too.

Leroy   It doesn't stop you charging into everything like a crusader and I'm the one at the back who can't get anything right, especially with Dwight.

Josephine   Don't you dare put that on me.

Leroy   It's like there is this secret to him that you won't share with me.

Josephine   There is no secret.

Leroy   He lets you in, in a way that he doesn't with me. I was good with Shirley, then when you started having concerns about Dwight, you shut me out. /

Josephine   That's because you didn't believe me. You wanted Dwight to be like Calvin.

Leroy   No parent ever gets it right. But you never let me get it wrong. You closed in ranks. You kept him to yourself. You stopped trusting me. Sometimes, I even think Shirley feels left out of your love.

Josephine   Shirley knows that I love her. /

Leroy   And I love Dwight too.

Pause.

Sometimes I catch Dwight staring at me like as if he's sizing me up or something. (*Beat.*) Like he knows something about me that I don't know. (*Beat.*) Like he senses all the things I feel and think and don't say. And he's waiting for me to say it.

Josephine   To say what?

Beat.

Leroy   That I'm jealous of him.

Josephine   What?

Beat.

Leroy   I'm jealous of my son. (*Beat.*) Of the way he is, of the way he feels everything, expresses everything, and stands firm, even against me.

Josephine   He's not against you. He just needs you to meet him where he is.

Leroy   I can't meet him when I don't know where I am. Lyons sucked out my pride out of my bones like marrow.

Josephine   That job was not the sum of who you are.

Leroy   It was my last anchor.

Beat. She leans in to touch him.

Prison Officer   No touching.

Josephine *doesn't let go of* **Leroy**'s *hand.*

Josephine   You've got to find what anchors you, Leroy. That's the only way you get out of the darkness.

Beat.

Leroy   Di darkes' part a di night –

Josephine   – a when day soon light.

Beat. She takes out a letter from her handbag.

Leroy   What's this?

Josephine   Dwight got a date for his review. Anna kick up a fuss bout Dwight an end up crying pan Granada.

Leroy   The world really do listen to crying white women. (*Beat.*) When is it?

Josephine   Fifteenth August. They're talking about a new diagnosis. Some developmental specialist has seen him.

Beat. They smile at each other. The **Prison Officer** *approaches.*

Prison Officer   Time's up.

Josephine *and* **Leroy** *stand. The* **Prison Officer** *pulls him away.* **Leroy** *waves to* **Young Shirley**. *He exits.*

Scene Seven

Meanwood Park Hospital, *August 1981*

Lights up on the hospital reception. **Young Shirley** *enters.*

Young Shirley   Anna's not here yet.

Josephine   Shirley, come sit down, you're making me nervous.

Young Shirley   I just want her to get here so that we can go in and get Dwight.

Young Shirley *sits.*

Josephine   Don't get your hopes up. You've seen for yourself how long and complicated things can get. This is just a meeting to talk about Dwight's assessment and what's next.

Young Shirley   What's it called again?

Josephine   Autism.

Young Shirley   Is Dwight going to be different now?

Josephine   No. (*Beat.*) You see how he moves and screams when he gets too happy or too sad?

Young Shirley   Yes.

Josephine   Well, this word tells the doctors, the police, the social, why he does it.

Young Shirley   So they'll be nicer to him now?

Josephine   Not all of them. He'll still need you to encourage him to use his words and express himself or else he'll shut down around all these strangers. He needs you and you need him. I've seen how sad you've been without him. You two best stick together even long after I'm gone.

Young Shirley   You're going to live forever.

Josephine At this rate I might just die in this waiting room if they don't come get us. What's taking so damn long?

Young Shirley (*laughs*) You said a bad word.

Josephine No I didn't.

Young Shirley (*mimics* **Josephine**) God hears and sees everything.

Josephine I don't even sound like that.

Beat.

Young Shirley Mum?

Josephine Yes.

Beat.

Young Shirley Does God really hear and see everything we do?

Josephine The eyes of the Lord are in every place, keeping watch on the evil and the good. Proverbs 15 verse 3. (*Beat.* **Young Shirley** *avoids making contact.*) Is there something that you want to tell me?

Young Shirley No. (*Beat.*) I'm just glad that God was watching over Dwight in here.

Josephine Me too.

Beat.

Young Shirley Mum?

Josephine Yes, Shirley.

Young Shirley Do you think Dad will miss me when he goes to Jamaica to see grandad?

Josephine Of course. But you can talk to him any time you miss him.

Young Shirley Will you miss him?

Beat.

Josephine I already do.

Young Shirley Don't worry, he'll come back to us. He has to, we're a family.

Beat.

Josephine So, what are you and Dwight going to do first if they say he can come home today?

Beat.

Young Shirley Mmmmm, play out with Calvin.

Josephine You like him, don't you?

Young Shirley Eurgh no. He's funny looking. /

Josephine Your dad was funny looking to me, until one day he wasn't. He became my best friend and I married him and had babies.

Young Shirley I'm not having babies with Calvin! Aliens might as well come down from space because it'll be the end of the world if I do.

Josephine Be nice to him. He likes you. He's always going to be right there, ready to save you even from aliens.

Young Shirley We're just friends, Mum.

Josephine Well, whomever you pick to do life with, make sure you pick wisely.

Anna *and* **Dwight** *enter.* **Dwight** *is wearing a new change of clothes and carrying his backpack.*

Young Shirley Dwight!

Young Shirley *rushes to him. He's a little apprehensive.*

Josephine (*to* **Young Shirley**) Give him a little space, Shirley. (*To* **Dwight**.) You've grown taller, son. Your new clothes suit you.

Young Shirley   I picked them out for you.

Josephine   That hair needs brushing though.

Anna   I tried but I don't think I was doing it right.

Young Shirley   I could do it.

Anna   Josephine, we should go in. Shirley, I thought you two would like to hang out in the family room.

Young Shirley   Okay.

Josephine (*to* **Young Shirley**)   Take my bag. There's a brush inside.

Shirley *takes it.* **Josephine** *and* **Anna** *exit. Beat.*

Young Shirley   D'you want to play the Adventure Game? (*Beat.*) We can use Mum's bag as the crystal. (*Holds it out.*) Here. You can decide where we hide it. (**Dwight** *inspects the bag before taking and smelling it. Beat.*)

Dwight   Estée Lauder.

Beat.

Young Shirley   She got a new bottle when we went to get your clothes. (*Beat.*) She said we all needed something new for a fresh start. I didn't want anything. (*Beat.*) I just wanted you back. (**Young Shirley** *is hoping for a response from* **Dwight**. *He continues smelling the bag. She starts mapping out the playing area.*) We can start the maze here and go all the way to the family room. I'll go see what they've got in there. (*She turns to exit and stops. She turns back around.*) Don't go anywhere, okay? Just wait here. I'll be back.

Young Shirley *exits.* **Shirley** *enters.*

Shirley   I thought having a brother meant I didn't have to fight over Mum's handbags.

Beat.

Dwight   She always smelt like flowers.

Shirley   She used to get me those little samples from Marks and Spencer to stop me stealing her perfumes.

Dwight   You used to steal her lipstick too, and my Sonic t-shirts and dad's cassettes.

Shirley   Alright, I wasn't some thief. It's borrowing when it's from family.

Dwight   You give things back when you borrow them.

Shirley   Says the person who took Dad's record player and never put it back in the front room.

Dwight   Mum said it was mine to keep. Dad didn't come back for it.

Beat.

Shirley   Fair enough. (*Beat.*) You stayed in your room a lot more when you had the music in there. You didn't even want to play the Adventure Game with me anymore.

Dwight   We can't stop change from happening, but we can try to prepare ourselves for it.

Shirley   Well, I wasn't ready for you to stop playing with me. (*Beat.*) I couldn't blame you though. I didn't want to play with you first sometimes. Calvin and Rachel were your friends too.

Dwight   Rachel was my girlfriend.

Shirley   You lie. When?

Dwight   When you went to university. Rachel kissed me. /

Shirley   That fast gyal made a moved on my baby brother!

Dwight   I'm not a baby. (*Beat.*) I'm a man.

Shirley   Yes, you are. (*Beat.*) I hope you two didn't, you know, you know what I don't even want to know if /

Dwight   We had sex. /

Shirley *covers her ears*

Shirley   Oh God, please stop!

Dwight   Uncle Curtis doesn't know.

Shirley   I'd like to rewind and not know either. (**Dwight** *laughs*.) It's nice to hear you laughing again. (*Beat*.) You've been shut down since Mum went into hospital.

Beat.

Dwight   I don't like hospitals.

Shirley   I know, that's why I didn't want you seeing her like that.

Dwight   I didn't say goodbye to Mum.

Shirley   I thought I was helping you by stopping you.

Dwight   You have to ask if I want help. You don't just start helping. It's rude. I don't like it.

Shirley   I'm sorry, okay. I'm really sorry. I just wanted things to be okay for you.

Dwight   Mum's dead. (*Beat*.) It's not okay.

Beat.

Shirley   I really miss her, D. I really miss her a lot.

Shirley *is visibly upset. Beat.* **Dwight** *approaches her.*

Dwight   I miss her too.

Dwight *holds her as she cries. Pause.*

Dwight *takes out the handbag from his backpack and hands her* **Josephine**'s *handbag.*

Shirley   Are you finally giving it back to me?

Dwight   It's the crystal.

Shirley   You want to play the Adventure Game now? We're in a church.

Dwight *starts hopping around.*

Dwight   Green, triangle, square, blue, triangle. Go, Shirley.

Shirley *follows his steps.*

Shirley   Oh, God. The kids at school would say I don't have the Meghan knees for this anymore.

Dwight   The time machine can take us back to earth and we can go home.

Calvin *enters and catches them playing.*

Calvin   You two seem good.

Dwight   We're playing the Adventure Game.

Calvin   I'm still jealous that you two never let me play.

Shirley *approaches* **Calvin**.

Shirley   It's a brother and sister game. Maybe we need to find another game that the three of us can play together.

Dwight   Four actually. Tanya likes games too.

Shirley   Who the hell is Tanya?

Calvin   Didn't the big man tell you?

Shirley   Tell me what?

Dwight   Man's got a girlfriend.

Calvin   She's outside asking if she can come in. She's worried about you, big man.

Dwight   Tanya likes to give me hugs when I'm sad.

Shirley   I bet she does.

Dwight   She's lovely. I'm going to marry her.

Shirley (*to* **Calvin**)   Did he just say /

Dwight *smiles at her.*

Shirley (*to* **Dwight**)   This woman has got some power. She can easily get you in and out of churches. (*Beat. She smiles at* **Dwight**.) Well, are you are ready to lay mum to rest now?

Beat.

Dwight   Yes.

Shirley *holds out his hand for* **Dwight**. *Beat. He takes it.* **Calvin** *exits.* **Shirley** *and* **Dwight** *exit.*

Curtain.